THE
AFTERMATH
of
FOREVER

THE AFTERMATH of FOREVER

How I Loved and Lost
and Found Myself.
The Mixtape Diaries

NATALYE CHILDRESS

The Aftermath of Forever
How I Loved and Lost and Found Myself
The Mixtape Diaries

Natalye Childress

Cover and book design by Meggyn Pomerleau

Published by Microcosm Pubishing, 2014

First Printing, June 1, 2014
ISBN 9781621067139
This is Microcosm #76143

Printed in the U.S. on post-consumer paper

Microcosm Publishing
2752 N Williams Ave.
Portland, OR 97227
www.microcosmpublishing.com

Distributed by IPG, Chicago
and Turnaround, UK

for
Jake Corbin,
who first told
me to take
my pain and
"write it out"

FOREWORD

By Jake Corbin

When I was in my mid-20s, I broke up with the first girl to ever hear me say, "I love you, too." She was getting ready to leave town, off to a university many cities away, and we knew the long distance thing wouldn't work. Although it was the logical decision, the whole ordeal wasn't easy; nothing ever is cold turkey. Like many young people in a committed relationship, we had done an amazing job at being inseparable. Our friends often referred to us as Eric and Donna from *That 70s Show*—not just because we were always side-by-side, but because I was scrawny with puffy hair and she was bigger than me and probably could've beat me up. It was a match made in sitcom heaven, but it was over. And when it was gone, everything I'd known for the last several years disappeared with it.

Now, most books of the romantic persuasion would end with us getting back together, or at least tease the thought before ending, but life and works of fiction rarely share the same story line. A lot of people break up and that's that. There's no going back to what once was. More specifically, we ended up more towards the "we almost forgot the other person exists" end of the spectrum. After sharing our lives for years, our relationship was abruptly reduced to a shoebox of mementos to be stashed away and forgotten.

As such, I reacted like many before me: I went to North Carolina for my cousin's wedding, got tanked on White Russians, met a cute girl from St. Louis, drunkenly repeated the same story over and over to her, was reminded of what I was doing each time, drank a margarita out of a glass cowboy boot, finally fell asleep, then threw up the next morning.

But guess what? We weren't even married! Breaking up sucks, even when it's mutual, but being cheated on and surprise divorced is mind-blowing. *The Aftermath of Forever* definitely has its fair share of NSFW details. The book is no holds barred in a way that is usually reserved for secret journals and therapy sessions, or at least a late-night conversation between good friends. But for all the juicy details and frank talk of sex, what has really been created is a document proving life can be pretty complex. From Internet dating and relationships via e-mail to internal struggles dealing with culturally-accepted female stereotypes, this book offers a modern day perspective that is entirely different from most other authors (i.e., men) in this genre.

What also jumps out in the pages of this book is just how damaging a break-up can be, especially divorce. In the case of the author, a change took place that isn't really addressed. All the ideas of no longer believing in true love or long-term relationships were there, but that was just talk. What's harder to put into words is how Natalye's personality changed; there was a spark missing. It wasn't always obvious, either, but every once in a while, in between the laughs, there was a quiet sadness that prevailed. That was never there before.

The other significant change post-matrimony was her selection process in regard to the opposite sex—it suddenly became very lenient. People are drawn to Natalye for her strong personality and ability to communicate both intelligently and with extreme sarcasm. She didn't put up with anyone's shit and spoke up if they tried to throw some of it her way. But during the period where this book takes place, we were often having conversations about whether she should call back a guy who followed up sex with being mean and ignoring her for weeks.

Everybody has their fair share of rebounds after a break-up, and Natalye was no different. The only problem was, dating a person or two isn't enough to get over having your heart stomped on and home life shattered. Natalye didn't just lose her relationship; she lost everything that went along with it. Thinking about having kids? Not anymore. What about owning a house? Can't afford it now. Settling down sure is nice, right? It used to be. So, of course, Natalye dated a few people. And, yes, a few of them were scumbags. But what can you expect when you're not looking for anything serious? Natalye wasn't looking to jump back into a relationship, and she ultimately attracted people with the same mindset. The way some of the boys treated her was pretty terrible, and she may have blown off a few herself, but it was going to end regardless. There was never a future with these boys, at least not the ones after her divorce. Like psychogenic amnesia's ability to block bad memories, Natalye's rebound relationships were a way of not dealing with the ongoing trauma from being crushed emotionally.

Looking back now, I guess I had it pretty easy. I definitely made a fool of myself in front of a few girls after my break-up, and managed to go out on a few things I called "dates." My fumbling attempts at flirting with the opposite sex weren't always well received, but I don't have much room to complain. I'm proud to report I eventually did meet my other half and have never been happier. Not only have we been married for a couple years, but she doesn't get too angry when I repeat the same story.

As luck would have it, Natalye hasn't done too bad for herself, either. Despite the heartbreak you're in store for with *The Aftermath of Forever*, rest assured that the dark cloud that followed Natalye around from time to time has been lifted; she's all jokes and dry wit again. Not only that, Natalye's belief in true love has been restored and is stronger than ever, thanks in no small part to her husband. And although he isn't the first guy to hear Natalye say, "I love you, too," he will be the last, and that's all that really matters. Sometimes the aftermath of what should have been forever ends up being the best part.

INTRODUCTION

Writing about sexual encounters and romantic experiences is certainly nothing new or groundbreaking. But there's also a reason why there is no shortage of people both writing and reading them. It's in our nature and our nurture. From day one, we immerse our minds in cultural manifestations of love—willingly or not. We read books about love and watch movies that end in happily ever after. We delight in the examples of lack's erasure and desire's fulfillment, believing that someday, we will find that happy ending for ourselves.

People in love tend to convince themselves that the love they experience will last forever. Otherwise, what is the point of entering into a committed, monogamous relationship? With the exception of the helplessly self-destructive or hopelessly narcissistic, conventional relationships should benefit both people involved in a mutual way. That is why we often enter into relationships with people who make us feel fulfilled. In that sense, love gives us purpose and validates our existence. At the same time, relationships function as mirrors to show us our own flaws and perfections in a particular context.

Like many, I've navigated romantic love, showing what happens to myself as a victim of this desire to love and be loved. But instead of looking at what happens when someone falls in love, I wonder what happens when the love that was supposed to last forever ends? How does it inform the view of our past? How does it affect the relationships that are to follow? More significantly, how do people cope with the aftermath of something that unexpectedly falls apart?

I once believed, perhaps naively, in this idealized version of love. Interestingly enough, although I was engaged to be married at 21, I knew it wasn't quite right. He was dishonest and I was distrusting, but I went through with it in spite of my hesitations, because a part of me believed I would never find someone who would love me again, and I rationalized that a half-assed version of love was better than none at all. And it is this valuation of myself, based on desirability that became engrained in me, that manifested itself again and again in relationships after my divorce. But instead of realizing that I shouldn't have married someone I had my doubts about, I began to let this person's treatment of me influence my own self-worth. During my three years of marriage, I came to define myself by my relationship, and as soon as that relationship came to an end, I no longer had a clear definition of who I was. As a result, when I began dating, I was lax with my criteria and careless in my choices.

Looking back on my writing as a collective whole, I note things that weren't apparent when I began this memoir, as well as aspects that, while evident to others, completely eluded me. These revelations had a lot to do with my misconception that I was writing about love when these stories are clearly about what I now consider the antithesis of love, or not-love.

It wasn't until my memoir was in front of me as a completed work that I saw the whole and not simply the parts. I thought I was writing about love, and in a sense I was, by focusing on what love wasn't, as seen through my actions as narrator. I sought out the first nine relationships—which in some part, can only be explained by the last—because, although I desperately wanted to find love, I was afraid, as the love I knew still fell short of the love I wanted. That doesn't justify the decisions made along the way, but it begins to explain them.

I learned that no relationship comes with a guarantee. With that in mind, I approached the relationships in this book as they were happening with the foresight that they might not work out. I knew just how painful break-ups could be, so as a protective measure, I reasoned that if I could avoid the kind of love that bonded people together and later broke them apart, I could avoid the inevitable heartbreak. So I opted to chase after the not-love, which I didn't realize was also an arduous path.

Surprisingly, swearing off love and notions of authenticity in these relationships was not the biggest challenge in store for me. While there were moments that my hopeful nature and jaded reality were at odds with one another, remaining nonchalant or noncommittal was relatively effortless. However, the real struggle was in accepting the hand I'd been dealt, a hand that I unwittingly stacked against myself. I put a particular vibe out into the world, and the universe answered in kind, serving up relationships and suitors who met me on my level. There is some truth in the idea that like attracts like, so it made sense that the emotional status of each man in this book was relatively on par with how I viewed myself at the time. As Stephen Chbosky wrote in *The Perks of Being a Wallflower*, "we accept the love we think we deserve."

Now, in hindsight, I have made an effort to piece together what that love has done to me in this book: a collection of short stories about significant loves, or perhaps, not-loves, in my life. Each chapter surrounds a particular individual and attempts to figure out what went right and ultimately, what went wrong. I found that the act of writing about my own affairs and indiscretions didn't serve to do away with the feelings of sorrow, anguish, confusion, or heartache I already experienced. It lessened them, it put them into perspective, but it didn't do away with the pain. Yet it seems the act of writing did serve some purpose, even if that purpose is unnamable.

I don't write about any of these ten men to remember them, or pay tribute to them, or even to point out their shortcomings with a laundry list compilation of how I was wronged. I wrote because it is the only way I can begin to grasp what happened and process it, as each of them functions as a lens, a way of examining myself. Yes, writers are often self-indulgent, and non-fiction writers especially can be seen as glamorizing their experiences. But my goal was to examine my (mis)steps in hopes of learning something about myself, bring about some sense of healing, and perhaps find some people that relate.

The downfall of this approach is that it can be seen as a harsh, unforgiving feminist manifesto demonizing the men I was with. There's an unequivocal lack of perspective from these men that makes them each unable to explain themselves or their thinking, or point out where I was to blame in the failure of our trysts. Because of this, even a sincere attempt to capture the most truthful snapshot of a relationship might strike the once-beloved as too candid, too skewed, too wrong.

Yet this critical approach serves a purpose. On one hand, in the majority of these relationships, the break-up or falling apart facilitated the lack of love on my part. On the other hand, it drew attention to the fact that what I offered was refused, because it wasn't enough for these men to love me. In the end, each relationship consisted of two people who were both desperately lacking, and that lack was fueled by a self-absorbed desire. It was less about desire for each other; instead, it was desire for something within ourselves to be fixed; our potentials realized.

And I willingly admit that I needed to grow. Though I might come across to many as cool, calculated, even cruel, I was largely broken. And in broaching this topic, I was attempting to put into play the part of myself that remained up in the air, the part that struggled between what I didn't have and how I sought to compensate for it.

Of course, part of my motivation was also to be my generation's version of Hank Moody, the brooding, sex-crazed author-protagonist in the television show *Californication*. I thought I could be the female answer to the brazen, sexually-deviant hedonist Tucker Max, author of *I Hope They Serve Beer in Hell*. But in exerting my own sexual agency, I realized it wasn't so easy to nonchalantly write and not somehow relive these experiences: the delight of the feeling of falling, the rapture of sexual conquest and pleasure, and the fear-laden disappointment and dismay of earth-shattering heartbreak. And since the majority of these relationships existed and subsisted with a reliance on alcohol to numb my true emotions, I made the decision to write without alcohol as an aid. Whereas I once used it as a desensitizer, numbing my feelings so I could face the pain, I decided to write facing these memories head-on—raw, open, exposed.

I found myself trying—really and truly trying—to recall all the details and make certain my narrative was a version of the truth. And then I hit my first and most notable roadblock: Unable to rely on alcohol, it hurt to write. I spent hours, staring at a blank page, a blinking cursor, the glow of white emptiness representing my open wound. This was my own lack, my unresolved broken-ness, staring back at me.

But eventually, I wrote through it. And when I was done, I realized that maybe I was no closer to discovering that love I so desperately hoped to find, but instead I turned inward and found something else: myself.

MAX

It was the beginning of the rainy season in San Francisco when Max and I began corresponding. I had broken up with a rebound and was sustaining myself with coffee, self-pity, and emotionally-charged journal entries. He wrote an anonymous blog about sexual escapism and I was intrigued. In our first exchange, he quoted Elliott Smith and I immediately found myself enamored of him in the most hyperbolic way.

On those dark October evenings I would lie in bed with the window open, listening to sad acoustic songs, not caring that the rain slanted in through the screen and splattered across the windowsill. Ever the dramatic, I thought I was done for, hopeless. But Max—he revived me. He breathed life into my nonexistent routine by giving me one. Or, at the very least, I had something to look forward to—a very unconventional sort of something.

Max lived a dual life, and few people knew about it. Even his significant other, a woman he never spoke of in specific detail, knew nothing of his secret split existence. It was one filled with discretion and deception, most of which was harmless, at least in the physical sense. He was an aspiring cheater who failed to follow through on his imagined infidelities. Max wasn't what you might call a sex addict, but he did have an above-average preoccupation with sex, which manifested in this secret life.

In the public sphere, he was a self-respecting businessman who dressed in slacks and a long-sleeved button-down everyday and made his way to the financial district, where he would spend eight hours sitting in an ergonomically sound office chair situated in an unimaginative office suite, with potted plants and an Alhambra water cooler in the corner. At least, this was the picture he preferred to paint. He had worked in radio for years, and found that what once was exciting and new had at some point become stifling. Eventually, he reached seniority status but was discontented with how little it offered him. He was making enough money, that's for sure, but he lacked the power to influence or instigate any kind of change, and as a result, he was dissatisfied.

In the private sphere, he was involved in a relationship that left him feeling trapped. He wanted to break it off, but lacked the courage to do so. Instead, he played out the "what ifs" in his head. He'd made up his mind that there was no way out, except straight through, and even the way there was laden with bumper-to-bumper traffic. Depending on how one looked at it, his relationship was either the unfortunate car stuck during commute time, or the pile-up itself. Max's only real escape—however temporary—was through writing, and that's where he and I intersected.

In the mornings, after an hour-long commute to the office, I'd wait for my computer to rouse itself out of its slumber while I brewed a fresh pot of coffee in the break-room. I was a journalist at the time, working for a real estate trade publication housed in a nondescript business park. When I was mentally prepared to face my job, or at the very least, awake enough, I'd settle down at my desk and take to sipping coffee while reading his emails, one of which was always waiting for me when I clicked on my inbox. They were typically candid in subject matter, with paragraph after paragraph of explicit sexual facts, thoughts, and desires.

There were the conquests: the girls he dated in the past, and how penetration with each one was exciting and new. He remembered intangible facts about them, like the way they smelled, or the sounds they made during orgasm. There were the fantasies: the Catholic schoolgirl scenario was prominent in more than a few of his visions, but he surprised me when he said that he wasn't interested in a threesome. Strange in my mind was the fact that he could stomach the thought of maintaining sexual relationships with two or more separate women, yet the idea of sharing sexual passion and desire between more than two people at the same time wasn't alluring, or even palatable.

"I passed by the most irresistible woman today on my way to work," one email might begin. "She was wearing a sweater tight enough that I could see her hard nipples underneath. We made eye contact, and all I could think about was taking her home, pulling up her skirt, and dipping myself into her sweet honey pot."

None of his fantasies were about me, however, as we were essentially strangers, save for our intensely overt and highly inappropriate keyboard dialogue. While he saw me as someone he could safely disclose his fantasies to, I used him as the sounding board for my broken heart. In that way, we functioned as makeshift therapists for one another; our relationship was a forum for honesty without fear of judgment.

Our emails to one another were punctuations throughout the paragraphs of our day. It wasn't until post-lunch when the correspondence would naturally taper off, as each of us had work to attend to, although we both had jobs that allowed us to toil only two or three hours each day, while performing cursory work for the remainder.

Max divulged to me his other vices, too: Strip clubs and the peep shows on his way home from work. I knew the details of his masturbation routine. How often he did it. What he thought about during. And his re-telling of those clandestine affairs made me a voyeur too. His words charged me, liberated me.

Every afternoon at four, I compiled the notes from the day's interviews with real estate executives and loan consultants and formed them into some semblance of an article. After clicking the save button three or more times to make certain I didn't lose any work before my Friday deadline, I'd put my computer to sleep, gather up my belongings and begin the 10-minute walk to the bus stop.

My bus, the 56, was a commuter route, so sometimes it ran ahead of schedule and sometimes it ran right on time. Most of the time, though, it was seven or eight minutes late, if not twenty. Regardless of when it arrived, Max seemed to call immediately after I had boarded and settled into my seat. He had this uncanny knack for getting the timing perfect.

Not wanting to disturb other riders, I'd talk in slow, hushed tones. Every time, he sounded happy to hear my voice, and I loved his—how playful it was, the rhythmic lilting of his words offset every so often by his seriousness.

"My day was boring," he'd begin with a sigh. "Work got crazy in the last couple hours. Sorry I didn't write you back."

"That's OK," I'd reply. "It was a welcome silence; I was able to file another story this afternoon, which means I can probably leave work early on Friday."

Sometimes, instead of talking about our days, we'd both tune out reality and talk about hypotheticals. We figured out that we only lived 30 minutes from one another; I was living in an apartment in the suburbs and he was located in the city by the bay. This proximity was perhaps the most exciting factor in our interaction. The fact that, at any moment, we could meet up and kick off some sort of lurid love affair. It was our very own watered-down erotic fantasy.

The possibilities were infinite, and as we grew closer, I begin to tease him.

"What if we played hooky and drove to a secluded beach and fucked?" I might write to him.

And there were the more mild proposals:

"Why don't we drive around town, without direction or purpose? We can listen to mellow indie rock and pretend for a couple hours that the songs are about us? Wouldn't that be nice?"

I always suggested the scenarios, and in turn, he urged me on, like it was a game—a dare.

It was during these conversations that I began to realize exactly the role I played in his life. It wasn't only his love life that was lacking; it was everything. I can't say for certain, but I think he hated his job slightly more than he hated his domestic situation. Because when an individual looks at things that closely, they all begin to meld together anyway, until it's too difficult to tell them apart. That's when a person begins projecting all the negative feelings about any and every thing familiar. I came to realize that he saved the best parts of himself for me. I was the one thing in his life that wasn't dying a horrible death.

Max always called me from a blocked number. I never once thought it strange that I didn't have his cell phone number, but I do admit I wondered how I was listed in his phone. I assumed he put me in as a fictitious person from work, or made it apparent that I was a journalist he knew, so he could talk his way out of any situation where his girlfriend might happen to see my name and number. Or maybe, I wasn't even in his phone. I liked that possibility too; it was exciting to imagine my number written down on some indiscriminate scrap of paper, which risked being discovered—or lost—at any moment.

As he talked, I imagined him walking up a slightly sloped sidewalk with a blur of houses in the backdrop. It was as though he was in a commercial, with a montage of San Francisco streets permanently situated in the background, which swept by at a slightly hurried pace. But each afternoon, it was someplace different. One day I imagined he lived in Potrero Hill, where he carried home a canvas bag full of groceries from the Whole Foods on 17th. The next day, it was SoMa, in a hip industrial loft adjacent to a tech-startup building with rent that was likely higher than a month's salary for me. And the following day, he lived in the picture-perfect Bernal Heights, tucked away from rushing city life and protected by the seclusion of its seemingly quaint residential atmosphere. One thing I noticed: The streets surrounding him were unfailingly quiet. Absent were the hustle and bustle of cars speeding by or ornery derelicts soliciting money. It was as though whatever environment he was in stopped for a moment in time and only the two of us existed.

Sometimes he called me on the weekends, when he was out with friends. Those were the times when it was unexpected. Typically, I'd be at the bar and have to excuse myself from whatever was going on around me. He'd be at a show of some sort with the guys and sneak outside with the excuse of a cigarette, or needing to call and check in with his girlfriend. But he called me instead.

From what I could gather about her, she was older, and a bit anal-retentive. She had a certain way of doing things that Max had likely found endearing in the early years, but had become annoying quirks. I pictured her as tall and beautiful, all legs, because it made me feel better about what he and I were doing. If I could make her into someone who was perfectly desirable but intellectually lacking, I could maybe substantiate my own role in his life.

Of course, what Max's role in my life was, I couldn't quite say. Months before, during the previous summer, the person I assumed I would spend the rest of my life with had cheated on me. Subsequently, when I confronted him, he left me. It was devastating, for he was the first and only person I had been in love with, and I thought that meant it would last forever.

As I began to mourn the loss of that love, something within me changed. It was gradual and unnoticeable at first, but eventually I found myself adopting apathy as a means of coping. Having never experienced real heartbreak prior, I wasn't prepared for the borderline-nihilistic after effects, in which I approached the idea of love as something without sacred moral boundaries. I found myself dismissing fidelity as a realistic option for any relationship. Getting mixed up in Max's world was a means of looking for answers to questions that had arisen in my life, namely why men cheat on their significant others and what type of women became home-wreckers. If I could place myself in the shoes of the unfaithful ex or his mistress, I thought maybe I could understand what I was missing.

And although Max wasn't my boyfriend or my lover, one day I made him a mix, as I so often do for the objects of my affection. While I am a writer and words are my primary means of expression, I have always felt as though language fails me. It's only with music—an intricate intermingling of crafted phrases and evocative sounds—that I can attempt to navigate the void where words stop working. In this manner—appropriating the words and music of others—I have always been able to find my way.

There is also something to be said about the art of the mix. It is like found poetry for music. Echoing the sentiment that "it's the thought that counts," I relish spending hours sitting in my bedroom and pouring over lyrics, determining the precise selection, arrangement and flow of songs to express my feelings. Each mix is different in content, medium, and intention, depending on the receiver. In Max's case, the songs addressed the infidelity that was so prominent in both our lives. But the mix itself was contradictory, made up of twelve songs full of proposed lyrical meaning yet lacking in real emotion. I felt everything and nothing for him, all at once.

"What's it for?" he asked, when I told him I'd emailed him a link to download the songs.

"It's for the boy who belongs to someone else," I said, with a doldrum-laden whimsy. I let my voice trail off. "If only we were lovers..."

ADD IT UP

Between the Bars – **Elliott Smith**
Middle Distance Runner – **Sea Wolf**
Ice Storming – **Aloha**
Your Rocky Spine – **Great Lake Swimmers**
We Are Nowhere and It's Now – **Bright Eyes**
Burn That Broken Bed – **Iron & Wine / Calexico**
Of Angels and Angels – **The Decemberists**
October – **Rocky Votolato**
Recycled Air – **The Postal Service**
Use Your Words – **Owen**
Lay Down Your Arms – **Flowers From The Man Who Shot Your Cousin**
Pity and Fear – **Death Cab For Cutie**

"You're special," he told me one day. "Different from other people. You're so smart, and you have so much to give."

I trusted him when he said this, even if I did wonder if there were others. Was I simply another name on a long list of routes to probable infidelity? Were there multiple women at one time, or did we all have our own place, running over and bleeding into the boundaries of one another? I'd like to think that it was I and no one else. I was the sole person, I convinced myself, whom he could be himself with.

As for the question of my own guilt: Did I feel bad that I was causing a man to emotionally cheat on his partner? The answer then was no. It wasn't that I was justifying my behavior in any sense, because I knew it was morally questionable, but I also knew that if it weren't me, it would just as easily be someone else. I happened to come along at the right time, which validated my own cynicism about love. Commitment was something I no longer found myself believing in, so the decision to be the emotional equivalent of the other woman was not something I contemplated all that much.

Why he stayed in that relationship, the one that made him so unhappy, I didn't know. I asked, and he produced half-assed, rehearsed answers about how hard it would be to leave. It wasn't until much later that I found out the extent of the complications, and what exactly kept him from leaving.

It wasn't her. It was her daughter. Max had ended up in a relationship with someone who wasn't a fit for him, but she had a child and Max was too attached to this girl who had attached to Max as her father.

"She's young," he told me. "But not so young that she doesn't know who I am. I practically raised her. She's like my own daughter. I love her as if she were."

"But you can have children with someone else," I said. "Why prolong something you don't think is going to last?"

"Why should my own selfish desire ruin her childhood?"

And he had a point, as paradoxical as it was. It was selfish of him to stay in the relationship when he was actively searching for something else. It was also selfish of him to leave because his sex life wasn't all he hoped it would be. So he stayed for the greater good of the child, whom he had grown to love as his own. Which maybe wasn't fair, or a good enough reason in my mind, but it was good enough for him.

Eventually, we did meet. One night in early December, more than two months after he entered my life, I stood on the dirty red cobbling of faux bricks designating the Civic Center and waited. I was in the middle of the sidewalk, situated next to a planter. I remember noticing the sun tuck itself behind the downtown skyscrapers and telling myself that if he took much longer, I'd have to seek refuge inside a nearby and warmer clothing store.

After what seemed like forever, my phone began to ring. I answered the call from a private number and as I did, I could feel the anxiety growing inside my chest.

"Hey," I said, attempting to sound nonchalant.

"Hey," Max echoed. "I'm almost there. Got held up at work. Where are you?"

"I'm on the sidewalk," I replied, scanning the crowd, uncertain of what direction he'd be approaching from.

"Are you next to a tree?" he inquired. "I think I can see you, leaning on it."

"That's me," I said with a smile, finally settling upon his face in the chaotic crowd of pedestrians. Though I only had a description to go by, the way his eyes zeroed in on mine, I knew exactly who he was.

"Bye," he said softly, hanging up the phone.

And then I looked up to see Max, entirely tangible and all too real, studying my reaction, his dark brown eyes peering at me through black frames. It was as though Tom Cavanagh and Jerry Seinfeld had melded together and stood directly before me, slightly breathless and sporting disheveled hair. In Max's case, he was a little bit lankier than I anticipated, and wore a messenger bag in lieu of the briefcase I'd imagined. He was older—in his late-30s—but he had the air of someone attempting to pass as a decade younger.

The assumption was that we were going to go back to his place. He had contacted me for that exact reason, and set up a meeting. The girlfriend was out of town on business and wouldn't be back for a few days. So we set out on a walk.

Our wayward path eventually led us to a spot near the Federal Building, where we sat down on a bench next to one another. The night had set in by this point, and the wind started up with bouts of rustling.

His voice was cautious and uncertain now. He wrote with such confidence, and spoke on the phone with such casualness, but something had changed. I guessed that the reality of what we were about to undertake overwhelmed him, and he realized it might be his only moment to back out before things went too far.

As he talked, I imagined pulling on his tousled hair as we made out in his bed, but I couldn't get myself into the moment. Something didn't quite add up. It wasn't an issue of chemistry, for there was between us an undeniable amount of intellectual attraction coupled with hardwired desire.

It suddenly struck me that he was the equivalent of the main character in *High Fidelity*, Rob Fleming—or rather, a not-yet-fully-realized version of Rob Fleming—who still lived off the fantasy of the woman in place of the real thing. And I knew that I could never be with someone like that, whether for a night or the span of a relationship, because he would forever lust after that ideal, non-existent woman.

After an hour of talking, we both stood up and said nearly simultaneously, "I should go." No discussion of us, no awkward moment. We both figured out that it wasn't the proper thing to do, for a multitude of reasons. Whatever prompted him to change his mind, I'd never know, but I was relieved that he did. As for me, I did my fair share of talking down fidelity, love, commitment, and all the associated words, but I also knew that

I respected her—this woman I never met and never would.

Max walked me to the corner of 7th and then turned and gave me a hug, before whispering a goodbye. I told him to have a good night, and we parted ways, me toward Market and he toward the neighborhood that, for me, would remain imaginary. And that was the first and last time we saw one another.

I still think about him on occasions, mostly on cold San Francisco mornings, when I am sitting in a coffee shop writing and thinking about the could-have-beens.

The problem with Max was that he was always in the process of becoming, but never being. Except for the little girl who kept him grounded, no one else took root in him. And eventually, that was what ended us. I think it was self-sabotage on his part. There wasn't any kind of discussion about it, even afterward—instead we slowly phased one another out of our lives, the time between emails becoming fewer and farther between until, eventually, they ceased.

On my part, it was a social experiment gone wrong, a first step in a series of missteps to discover if love truly existed. I wanted to live outside the version of myself that I'd built up, the one who could be counted on to do the proper thing. I wanted to see if being reckless paid off more than playing by the rules.

It turned out that Max was the one too afraid to live outside himself. Maybe that's how the fantasy was created: with a realization, whether conscious or not, that it was just that: a fantasy, an escape, a few hours a day when he could feel like he wasn't stuck.

VAN

"And how was your night last night?"

The sternness of the voice asking startled me from my light sleep, making me wonder where I was. I opened my eyes, blinking quickly to adjust to the daylight. Standing over me was my older brother, his arms crossed, assuming a faux-reprimanding stance. I pulled my sleeping bag over my head, groaning.

"That good, huh?"

"Yeah yeah," I grumbled.

He walked into the adjoining kitchen, continuing to talk, oblivious to my desire to forego the gossiping and go back to sleep.

"So this Van guy, which one is he again?"

Grudgingly, I poked my head out from underneath the sack.

"He's, you know, a guy I used to date."

My brother stood with his back to me, pouring freshly brewed coffee into a cup.

"You want some too?"

"Duh."

"I don't have any soy milk, so you'll have to drink it black," he said, handing me a steaming cup as I crawled out of the sleeping bag and situated myself, cross-legged, on the bedroom floor of his studio apartment.

I took a deep breath, knowing I couldn't lie to my brother.

"I was dating Van back when you lived in the apartment with Ant and Jen. I kind of, um, gave it up to him."

I studied his reaction as I spoke, noticing his unsuccessful attempt to mask surprise.

"Smith wasn't my first," I said exasperatedly, referring to the boy who was, at one point in the not-so-distant past, the love of my life. This was something I'd figured he already knew, but judging by the look on his face, prior to my revelation, it had only been a mild suspicion at most.

"I was boning him way before Smith and I started dating," I said matter-of-factly.

I paused to take a sip of coffee.

"And don't worry," I said, lifting the cup to my lips. "You'll get to meet him today. He left his cell phone in the backseat of my car, so I have to return it to him in an hour."

Three or four years had passed since I'd last seen Van. After our whirlwind relationship, I never thought I would see him again. That's not to say I didn't think of him from time to time, but since I settled down with someone else, there seemed to be no point for us to connect again.

This changed a month prior, when my relationship had gone awry. The breakup was as big and messy as they come, but instead of drowning myself in sorrow, I decided to take a more hedonistic approach, instead, drowning myself in alcohol and gratuitous sex.

It was the Fourth of July weekend, I was in the Silicon Valley visiting my brother, and nothing seemed more apropos than celebrating my newfound freedom by acting it out. It wasn't a challenge to get in touch with Van either, and after informing him that I was single and wanted to see him, he agreed to meet up.

At the time, it felt like coming full circle, meeting up with Van again. In retrospect, some small part of me wanted to relive my experiences with the first boy I'd had sex with, and to attach meaning to a memory, in an attempt to protect it.

I always thought my first time would be with someone I loved. Although the details weren't meticulously planned out and I had yet to know who would take my virginity, I had promised myself I would only give it up for someone who meant something to me.

I hadn't always felt that way. Raised in the Christian faith, years and years of youth group had engraved in me the doctrine of no pre-martial sex. Having sex was giving away a part of yourself that you could never get back. And I believed that. To some extent, I still believe that. The difference is that back then, I was also scared of sex. To combat that fear of the unknown, I committed to protecting my virginity. I wore a purity ring. I even participated in "True Love Waits" conferences, where thousands of youth group kids would convene for six weeks in Sunday School classrooms across the country, pledging to remain chaste until marriage. In return, we were all given CDs with songs by Christian artists like Newsboys, Steven Curtis Chapman and DC Talk, the lyrics of which all spoke to the importance of remaining pure. What I didn't realize then is that this true love I'd been told about didn't ever really exist. At least not in my world.

As I got older and found myself exposed to the normal teenage temptations, I still resisted having sex. Not because I was afraid of it, but because I began to respect it. My ideology evolved as the reasons for abstinence became different, and more complicated. I no longer cared about "saving myself" so much as examining the intention behind sex. I couldn't have said at 16 whether or not I would wait until I was married, but I definitely knew I wanted my first time to be with someone I loved, who cared about me. It was strange; I wasn't naïve enough to believe in waiting until marriage, but I was naïve enough to think that there might be such a thing as a soul mate.

When Van came along, he didn't strike me as "the one," but he definitely was right on par with my place in life. He was a PK, or Pastor's Kid, an abbreviation well known in the church community. From the moment he revealed this fact to me, we both knew it meant something more than face value. PKs tended to be resistant to their strict religious upbringing, and resentful of the close scrutiny their position entailed. Everything they did—whether good or bad—reflected directly on their parents.

So naturally, many of them rebelled. It was the only way they seemed able to separate from their parents.

Our meeting was unconventional, in that we were strangers who connected through the Internet. This was in the early 2000s, back when meeting people online was just beginning to become practice. I hadn't met up with anyone who wasn't somehow connected to someone in my real life, be it through a friend of a friend or musical circles, because I was skeptical about what someone's intentions might be.

It was December of 2004, maybe a week before Christmas. I had driven down to San Jose to visit my brother, but his work schedule kept him busy, so I hung out in his apartment with little to do. Van, with whom I'd started an email correspondence shortly before out of boredom and curiosity, lived nearby. He worked at a restaurant in San Francisco and his social networking profile said he liked the band Coco Rosie, so I figured he was harmless.

I stood out on the circle in front of my brother's apartment complex and waited for him to arrive. I was anti-cell phone at the time, so I'd left a note for my brother, in case I returned after he did.

Before my nerves could get too jittery, a maroon car that looked slightly beat up, just as Van had described, pulled into the complex and stopped next to me. I took a deep breath and opened the door and stepped into the passenger seat.

"Hey," I said confidently.

"Hi. Where do you want to go?"

"Anywhere. Away from here."

So we started driving.

I don't remember any details from the drive, other than it was aimless and we talked and talked. I was depressed. He had already known that. And it felt nice to share that part of myself with someone, without feeling judged. I was sick of the medication, the therapy appointments, and the concerned looks. It was refreshing to be somewhat anonymous.

In turn, he used me as a sounding board for his own struggles. He had been an accomplished basketball player in his younger years, and he knew how much it disappointed his father that he was more interested in rock-climbing than pursuing team sports. He managed a successful restaurant in San Francisco, but what he really wanted was to be a filmmaker—again, a route for which he felt no support.

He took me around the Silicon Valley via various freeways, pointing out locations of minor consequence: his high school, his favorite restaurant, and the exit he took to go to the gym.

After an hour of driving, he took an exit for Cupertino and turned down a quiet side street. He pulled up to a gated community and rolled his window down.

"What are you doing?" I asked inquisitively.

"Just checking something."

He punched in a five-digit code and the gate opened.

I tossed him a confused look. He smiled.

"I used to live here," he said. "When I was younger. Turns out they haven't changed the code in all these years."

He inched the car forward and turned right, driving a couple hundred feet before settling into a parking space under a tree. The walls of the community towered over the car and there were no streetlights, leaving us obscured by darkness.

Van unbuckled his seatbelt and I did the same. He opened the driver side door.

"Come on," he said.

I climbed out and walked around to the other side. He opened the backseat door for me in a gentlemanly gesture, and I crawled back into the car. No sooner had the door slammed shut then he turned and kissed me.

I reached up and caressed his face, then moved back to look at him. Placing my hands on either side of his neck, I grabbed his hair and pulled him close to me, inhaling the scent of weed and laundry detergent.

"What are we doing?" I whispered.

Not answering, he kissed me once more, which was answer enough. I felt like I was in high school all over again.

As his hands began to explore, I looked him in the eye.

"No sex," I said firmly.

He nodded to acknowledge he'd understood, but proceeded to take off my shirt and unbutton my pants. I smiled knowingly and took control, pushing him off me and climbing on top. Taking a tip from all the issues of *Cosmopolitan* I'd read, I started at his lips and kissed my way down his body, using my hands to keep him hard. And after I was done sucking him off, I swallowed, which not only drove him wild, but also surprised him.

"Why did you do that?" he asked, astounded.

"What, South Bay girls are spitters?"

"No. Well, kind of. Yes. But. You didn't have to do that!"

"I wanted to. Besides, where was I going to spit? On your floor mat?"

He smiled and pulled me in for another kiss. We cuddled up in the backseat for another five or ten minutes. Finally, I broke the silence.

"It's getting late..."

"...Yeah I should probably get you back before your brother starts to worry."

He drove me back to the complex. Before I got out, I gave him another kiss.

"Don't be a stranger," I said.

Later that night, as I lay on the living room couch trying to sleep, I replayed the sequence of events in my mind, a smile plastered on my face as I drifted off. What I wouldn't realize then, or until years later, was how backward I seemed to have everything. Maybe it was my religious upbringing, maybe it was the influence of the media, or maybe it was a combination of both (or none) of those things, but the act of oral sex—it was psychologically separate from sex, and mostly meaningless to me.

The weeks that followed were filled with random chats on instant messenger and emails between the two of us. I got a cell phone for Christmas and we texted one another regularly.

Yet, conversations about "us" were minimal, mostly centered on when we'd see one another next. A relationship was not what either of us had in mind, considering the distance and our scattered mental states. We were admittedly both depressed for our own reasons, but figured a pseudo-relationship couldn't hurt.

It was six weeks before we saw one another again. On my way out of town after another weekend visit, he called me up and we decided to meet in a parking lot off the Foothill Expressway. Van was already there when I arrived, leaning nonchalantly against the side of his car. When I pulled up next to him, I opened the door and was immediately met with an embrace, his mouth wasting no time in seeking out mine.

"Get in," he said to me, holding open the door.

I didn't need any convincing.

"Go ahead and put on some music."

While I fiddled with my iPod, he took off driving up the expressway, through Los Altos Hills and up into the Santa Cruz Mountains.

He shifted his car around the corners with his left hand, just so he could hold my hand with his right. My musical selection, Brandtson's "Dial in Sounds," played on his stereo as we raced up to the highest point in the road and pulled into a dirt and gravel-filled lot.

"Hurry! Quick!" he said excitedly.

He ran around to my side of the car and grabbed my hand, leading me up the peak of the mountain. We arrived at the summit and he stood still, looking toward the West without a word.

I followed his gaze just in time to catch the sun spreading across the sky in front of us. Moments later it was gone from our sight, but the horizon maintained pure brilliance for nearly twenty minutes.

He took my hand once again, this time leading me to the grassy expanse that stretched between the car and us. We sat down and he put his arms around me, kissing me.

"I've missed you," he whispered in my ear.

His hand crept down and unbuttoned my pants in a familiar way, his fingers gliding underneath and into my wetness. He took off my pants—his were next. I didn't protest. And gently, quickly, before I could react, he slid his hard cock into me and began thrusting. And like that, my virginity was gone.

After he came, we lay back in one another's arms, smiling and laughing to ourselves. But all I could think was about how I'd had sex. It was difficult to wrap my head around, namely because it hadn't turned out like I once expected—I wasn't married and I wasn't in love with him. But there were no negative emotions floating around. Instead, my head felt ethereal, inebriated. I was the same person, but not.

The sky was completely dark, except for the light of the stars and the moon, so we pointed out the constellations we knew to one another. And when we ran out of them, he helped me up and held my hand as we walked through the nighttime to find the car.

Back in the Honda, we drove alongside the top of the mountain ridge on Highway 9 until we reached an open vista. He asked if I minded if he smoked a bowl. I did not. Parked, we sat in the car and looked East, over the entire Bay Area spilling out before us. I could see San Jose to the right of me, Palo Alto in front of me, Oakland in the distance, and San Francisco hiding in the lower left corner. The lights were flickering and the buildings were nearly impossible to make out, but we could easily identify the main bridges connecting the bay and the prominent hills encompassing South City, and if we looked out on the other side of the road, behind us, nothing but mountains and the coast.

In the months that followed, we met up a few more times, each encounter more sexually-charged than those that came before, my own sexuality now conflicted but finally free. Where once there was fear, guilt, and shame at the thought of sexual pleasure, my attitude toward sex transformed, and I found myself reveling in the physical. There was the car sex, which by nature of fear of discovery, was quick and fun. There was the night I snuck into his parents' house just past midnight, when he pressed my mouth into a pillow as he entered me from behind, in an effort to keep my moans from waking his brother in the next room. These moments were intense, dramatic, and the absolute best thing I could have hoped for from the boy who took my virginity.

But there was something missing, and as we both took steps toward mental clarity, we began to rely on one another less and less. There was never a clear break-up or a definitive moment when we stopped seeing one another. We simply grew up and apart.

While I sometimes found myself pining for him, I somehow knew—although I refused to admit it to myself at the time—that my attachment to Van didn't stem from feelings of love, but rather from physical intimacy. And although I played off sex as nothing special, part of me wanted him to mean something more to me, so much so that I tried to convince myself we had a future.

I even went so far as to construct a playlist of songs that made me think about him. Some were formulaically hopeful, others were romantically desperate, and the remainder communicated the feelings I couldn't pinpoint on my own. I was all at once conflicted and confused, wanting desperately to feed the pretense that I had found happiness in something, in someone, when that was far from the truth. I was lost, and I wanted Van to be my grounding point, but for all of the wrong reasons.

And for a while, the charade worked. Driving around in my car, listening to these songs, I could convince myself for forty-five minutes or an hour that he and I were more than we were, that our relationship was something normal and real.

I JUST FEEL FREE
AND A
LITTLE BIT EMPTY

Take It Easy (Love Nothing) – **Bright Eyes**
One Evening – **Feist**
We're at the Top of the World (To the Simple Two)
The Juliana Theory
Take Me Anywhere – **Tegan & Sara**
Slow Hands – **Interpol**
Just Tonight – **Jimmy Eat World**
I Wasn't Prepared – **Eisley**
Storm & Stress – **Bloc Party**
Somewhere Only We Know – **Keane**
Butterscotch – **Coco Rosie**
Mark It A Zero – **Brandtson**
Portions for Foxes – **Rilo Kiley**
Runaway – **Mae**

These thoughts began to run rampant when I made the impulsive decision to seek Van out all those years later. And when we met up, it was as though nothing had changed. This time, though, we were in the backseat of my car instead of his.

The following day, when I returned his cell phone on a random, pre-selected street corner, I was struck by how little I felt about him. I didn't think seeing him would reignite all the feelings from years before, but somehow I thought such a symbolic step would make me feel something. Instead, as I introduced him to my brother and watched them shake hands, I felt like an outsider to my own life, watching someone who wasn't me going through the motions. I realized then that there could no longer be any backward movement in my life. From there on out, I had to keep pressing forward, because it was the only way I would find myself. After handing over his phone, I hugged Van and said goodbye, knowing that this time, it was for good.

"Happy Fourth of July," I called over my shoulder as I walked away. Independence Day.

CHAZ

Chaz was out of my league. With his smooth, angular face framed by perfect brown locks, he was the kind of guy who could grace the cover of a magazine. In addition to looks, he appeared to have every other detail of his life worked out: a flashy sports car, a college degree, a steady paycheck, and an apartment of his own in the middle of a city. With all these things, I never imagined that I could be a part of his life, much less an accessory on his arm. Yet every woman has that unattainable guy on her list that she crushes on, pines for, and lusts after—in spite of the odds.

A former frat boy, he'd attended Chico State, a university notorious for its party lifestyle and copious beer consumption. He had a way with women, and always knew just what to say. You know the type: the one who, when you're talking with him, makes you feel as though you're the only other person on the planet. That's how Chaz was. Except for whatever reason, I was able to call Chaz mine, if only for a while.

We met in the summer while I was on a break in my undergraduate career, working at a newspaper in the automotive advertising section, and trying to figure out what I wanted to do with my life. The circumstances surrounding our meeting were nothing out of the ordinary. He was the new guy at work who had recently graduated with his bachelor degree and was ready to join the professional ranks. On his first day in the office, during our weekly meeting, the higher-ups briefly introduced him. But I'd noticed him before that.

My first impression was that he was intimidatingly good looking, but I was shy and uncertain, lacking in self-esteem. As a result, I always opted for the more passive routes of flirtation than ones that forced me to step outside my comfort zone. Besides, I was always infinitely more charming with my words. So instead of going up to his cubicle and introducing myself to him, I sent him an email welcoming him to the company and giving him a quick orientation as to what was up. I followed it up a bit later with an in-person hello, and found his attitude disarming. He was aware of how attractive he was, but exuded a warm and friendly attitude, which suggested he didn't have an over-the-top ego. So in spite of being skeptical of this smooth talker who drove an Orange Mustang Cobra convertible and was definitely not my type, I was too intrigued to stay away.

Initial introductions taken care of, it wasn't long before Chaz and I moved from co-worker territory to friend territory. As there were only a few of us in the office who were under the age of 40, we naturally bonded. Every morning around the same time, he'd swing by my cubicle—which was conveniently located on his way to the back door—and interrupt my work. I was usually on the phone with an account, so he'd loiter in the background until my conversation ended.

"Wanna get some coffee?" he'd ask cheerfully, the moment I hung up.

"You know it," I'd respond, throwing my headset onto the desk and grabbing my key card.

Then, off we'd go, out the door and through the parking lot, jay-walking across B Street to the front of the mall, which contained our closest coffee shop.

It became a routine for us, as were our semi-weekly lunches. More often than not, we'd grab a booth at the kosher deli on 4th Street, and sit and talk through our hour-long lunch break, sometimes infringing upon the two-hour territory. We were both ambitious workers, and lucky enough to not have a micro-managing boss, so in most cases, no one missed our presence.

It was during those times together that I really got to know Chaz as more than just the pretty boy. He was smart and savvy, put-together and skilled at navigating social situations. But there was also another part of him that few people knew. It wasn't that he was insecure, but he was human: susceptible to feeling weak or sad or used. When I told him about the boys I was innocuously dating, he told me all about the girls he wined and dined, but I could tell there was a longing for something more underneath, though he never quite admitted it.

But true to his alma mater, he was still a party animal. Meanwhile, I wasn't yet 21, and while my older siblings had been supplying me with alcohol for years, drinking still remained a bit of a novelty. So having a 26-year-old man procure drinks for me wasn't something I was opposed to. Naturally then, our hanging out extended into the after-work hours, and once every couple weeks I would drop by his place. We'd snack, drink beer, and watch movies or talk. Sometimes, we'd even cruise around town in his Mustang, fighting over control of the stereo.

"Let's listen to Madonna," he'd say, inserting *The Immaculate Collection* in his CD player.

"Naw," I'd object, trading the disc in favor of some Duran Duran. "You concentrate on driving. I'll pick something to listen to."

This back-and-forth with music was a regular topic of contention, which I finally suggested we fix with a mix meme I'd recently stumbled across.

"Your life is a movie," I began, spelling out the hypothetical scenario. "And each scene needs to have music. So pick what song plays at what moments. It's like your coming-of-age soundtrack. I'll make one for you of my life, and you make one for me of your life."

This is what I ended up with:

MOVIE SOUNDTRACK

Opening Credits: *Seventeen Years* – **Ratatat**

Waking Up: *Between Us and Them* – **The Moving Units**

Car Driving: *Bohemian Like You* – **The Dandy Warhols**

High School Flashback: *Bad Scene, Everyone's Fault* – **Jawbreaker**

Nostalgic: *You Remind Me of Home* – **Benjamin Gibbard**

Bitter/Angry: *Fractions* – **Emery**

Break-Up: *Rough Draft* – **Yellowcard**

Regret: *How Can You Be Sure?* – **Radiohead**

Nightclub/Bar: *Boys and Girls* – **Blur**

Sad/Breakdown: *Look Up* – **Stars**

Funeral: *Every Shining Time You Arrive* – **Sunny Day Real Estate**

Mellow: *Let Your Head Hang Low* – **Aloha**

Dreaming About Someone: *Drawing a Line in the Sand* – **Brandtson**

Sex: *Take it Easy (Love Nothing)* – **Bright Eyes**

Contemplation: *Chimera Obscurant* – **The Velvet Teen**

Self-Discovery: *The First Single* – **The Format**

Falling in Love: *Closer to Mercury* – **Wheat**

Friends: *Wonderful People* – **Q And Not U**

Closing Credits: *AM 180* – **Granddaddy**

As for Chaz's mix, he opted for a healthy combination of 80s and 90s hits, with a deep cut or two thrown in for good measure.

MY LIFE, VOL. 1.

Opening Credits: *Today* – **The Smashing Pumpkins**
Waking Up: *Youth of the Nation* – **P.O.D.**
Car Driving: *Freedom 90* – **George Michael**
High School Flashback: *When I Come Around* – **Green Day**
Nostalgic: *Freshmen* – **The Verve Pipe**
Bitter/Angry: *Zombie* – **The Cranberries**
Break-Up: *Return of the Mack* – **Mark Morrison**
Regret: *Nobody Knows* – **Babyface**
Nightclub/Bar: *You Shook Me All Night Long* – **AC/DC**
Sad/Breakdown: *Purple Rain* – **Prince**
Funeral: *November Rain* – **Guns N' Roses**
Mellow: *Wicked Game* – **Chris Isaak**
Dreaming About Someone: *Yellow* – **Coldplay**
Sex: *Justify My Love* – **Madonna**
Contemplation: *Come Undone* – **Duran Duran**
Falling In Love: *Now That I Found You* – **Terri Clark**
Friends: *Player's Holiday* – **T.W.D.Y.**
Closing Credits: *Into the Mystic* – **Van Morrison**

Even though the music wasn't necessarily what I listened to, I played his CD in my Discman while I drove around in my beat-up car. And although he forgot to include the track about self-discovery, I appreciated that he didn't repeat any of the artists on the mix.

How we eventually evolved from friends to more than was something neither of us could clearly explain, except that there seemed to be an all-too-natural progression of events. There was sexual tension between the two of us, no doubt about that. But it had remained unvoiced and unexplored for a long time. So though I was surprised, I hardly even flinched when Chaz sent me an email at work one day that hinted at making things physical. Considering our work email was constantly monitored, the discourse was disguised with plenty of euphemisms, but I saw through them. After we exchanged a handful of messages, he ended with one that read: "Stop by tonight and we'll see what happens."

Upon receiving it, I jumped up from my chair and made my way toward his desk, determined to figure out if he was serious. In the interest of protecting my ego, and because I was still relatively insecure, I needed to confront him in person. But when I made it to his cubicle, he wasn't there.

"Where's Chaz?" I asked a co-worker.

"Chaz? Oh he left early, hon," she said. "Dentist appointment. Something I can help you with?"

"Nawww," I said, shaking my head in disbelief, before my lips curled into a knowing smile. "It can wait."

That evening, I parked in the lot adjacent to his apartment on Second Street and walked up the steps with a mixture of trepidation and thrill. As I knocked on the door, I took one last moment to fiddle with my outfit, which was casual, yet not lacking intention. I was wearing a new pair of jeans, just for the occasion, but still dressed comfortably, not wanting to come across as eager.

Moments after I knocked, I heard footsteps, as Chaz made his way to the door. I took a deep breath, and then it opened.

"Hey darling," he said, giving me a hug.

"Hey," I smiled back.

"Heineken?"

"Yes please."

I dropped my bag down next to the kitchen table. He strolled over to the fridge and in one even movement pulled out a beer, popped off the top, and handed it over.

"I'm listening to Joy Division," he said, as he walked over to the couch and took a seat. Then, cocking his head inquisitively, his bangs falling in his eyes, he looked over at me. "You like them, right?"

"I love Joy Division," I said. "But New Order always wins in my book."

I hesitated in the kitchen for a moment before making my way over to the living room and sitting down next to him.

"No movie tonight?" I questioned.

"No," he said. "I mean, we can watch one if you want."

"I think movies are the only things we tend to agree on," I said.

"Are you kidding me?!" he asked incredulously. "I think we agree on most everything. Well, except music. You're too pretentious." I laughed, and then nodded, realizing he was right.

"We both love 8os though," I conceded. "So your taste *could* be worse."

"I need to fucking smoke," he said, grabbing his pack and lighter from the coffee table. "Want to join me outside?"

"No thanks," I replied, and shrugging, he made his way through his bedroom and out onto the balcony.

Meanwhile, Ian Curtis was singing about "Unknown Pleasures," which was remarkably apropos. I sunk back into the couch, which was really just an upright futon bed, and sipped on my beer, listening to the music and hoping the combination of the two would curb my nervousness.

A few minutes later, Chaz came back in the room and plopped onto the couch, positioned purposely closer to me than usual. He looked at me with a seriously playful look in his eyes, and flipped his hair confidently. Without a word and with only a hint of a smile, he leaned down and kissed me.

The cigarette smoke lingered upon his lips. I placed my right hand on the side of his face, and then grasped onto the back of his neck, as he took his arm and pulled me over onto his lap. I began kissing his jawline, making my way up along the curve of his face, to his ear.

I moaned softly, as I began sucking on his lobe. That seemed to do the trick, because he took his left hand and made his way up under my shirt, unclasping my bra in under a second.

For an hour, I sat this way, on his lap, legs wrapped around him, as we explored one another's bodies. There was no pressure on his part to do more than I wanted, and he didn't even hint at the idea of having sex, knowing it was something I wasn't ready for.

At the end of the evening, as our kisses slowly tapered into cuddling and talking, I took a deep breath.

"Chaz," I began. "What is it? You know, about me. What do you see in me?"

He opened his eyes and looked into mine.

"You're fucking adorable," he said, without skipping a beat.

As the following week progressed, we grew closer, and our relationship evolved to the point where I was over there almost every night until two or three in the morning. We stayed up late making small talk and broaching controversial topics too, as Chaz was always one to play devil's advocate. He argued with me over any and every thing, sometimes just because he could— but mostly because he loved to infuriate me when he was right.

"Chaz," I told him one day in early February. "I think I want to have sex with you."

It was then that I explained to him my relationship with Van. He'd known I was seeing someone else casually, but it hadn't mattered because Chaz and I were just friends who occasionally made out. But the weekend before was when I'd lost my virginity, and feeling a bit more confident about myself, I told Chaz I wanted to explore my sexuality with him.

"Really?" he responded, eyes wide with excitement. But then he stopped. "Really?" he asked again, with a concerned look on his face. "I don't want you to do something you're not comfortable with."

"Yes," I said. "I want to experience it. And I want to experience it with you. I mean...I trust you. And we care about one another."

So it was decided. I wanted sex to be a healthy and positive experience, and Chaz was the ideal partner. He was well versed in the art of pleasing women and knew what he was doing, having had plenty of partners. He was—more importantly—my friend. And goddamn, he was sexy.

Beforehand though, there were things we needed to discuss. Both of us were clean, we made certain of that. And a few ground rules. We always had to use condoms. We were allowed to sleep with other people. We weren't required to tell one another if there was someone else, but protection was a must. Either of us could call it off at any time we wanted.

It all felt highly clinical to some degree, this planning out of sex, but it made sense. I was proud of myself, for being communicative and honest about my intentions and expectations. And when I arrived at his house a day after we mapped it all out, it felt like just another evening together. He had already begun a movie, *The Tao of Steve*, which I'd never had much of an interest in watching, despite recommendations from friends. Still, I sat down next to him and drank a beer, attempting to get involved in the plot.

After a half-an-hour, I gave up.

"This shit's boring," I said, sighing.

"Let's go in my room instead."

He led the way, with me trailing behind. I crawled onto the bed and we began making out and taking off one another's clothes, until we were both naked. He stroked my forehead with his hand and kissed me, smiling. I opened my legs to take him in.

"God, you feel so fucking good girl," he told me, once he was inside me.

The thing with Chaz that made our relationship so great for me was our communication. In the week or two that followed, we not only had sex all the time, but we talked about it all the time. In the past, I'd experienced physicality as something that existed only in a certain space in time, with all conversation relating to it taking place in that isolated zone. But with Chaz it was all-relevant. Arguably, this was because our sex was so indiscriminate, but realistically, it was because we were both adults, doing an adult thing and talking about it in an adult way. So a week or two after we'd started hooking up, it was no surprise when he broached the topic in the middle of the afternoon.

"I wanted to talk about something with you," he said, walking over to what he referred to as his goody drawer. He wasn't like most guys with a goody drawer full of sex toys. No, Chaz had *two* goody drawers. He opened the top one, rifled underneath a pile of handcuffs and cock rings, took something out, slammed the drawer shut, and tossed what he'd taken out over to the couch, where I was seated.

"What's this?" I asked him, picking it up with hesitation.

"It's a sex book," he said, matter-of-factly.

"What, like the *Kama Sutra*?"

"No, but I've got that too, if you want to look through it."

"I'm good," I said, laughing. "But what's this all about?"

"It's for us," he said, taking a seat beside me and putting his arm around my shoulders. "Open it up."

I turned the first few pages until I reached the table of contents.

"It has ideas to spice things up in the bedroom," he said. "Read through them, find what aligns with your fantasies, and we'll try them out."

I smiled.

"Really?" I asked. "Are you serious? What about your fantasies?"

"This is all about you," he said reassuringly. "Don't worry about me. I'm easy to please. But I want this sex to be good for *you*."

I couldn't complain. I'd stumbled across every female's dream come true. It was like having my own sexual slave who was not only eager and willing, but also totally capable of pleasing. And he was extremely witty and incredibly charismatic to boot.

But still, I couldn't help but feel that things were too good to be true. This was a hugely sought after guy who, although he was casually involved with me, seemed to be seeing only me.

I was relieved then, when he told me one day that he had a date scheduled for that night. I had been doing my best not to become attached, because somewhere in the back of my mind, I believed what I'd been telling myself the whole time: that he was out of my league, that I was not good enough for him. As much as I wanted to be swept up in the fantasy of me and Chaz, I mentally tried to prepare myself for the worst so that I wouldn't be disappointed. And finally he was seeing someone else, a fact that validated all I'd been telling myself.

"Who is she?" I asked playfully.

"Just some chick I met."

I didn't press him for further information, knowing that his use of the word "chick" meant she didn't mean anything to him—or at least, not anything like I meant to him. I told him to enjoy himself and that I'd see him the next day.

That evening, my phone rang. The name on the screen was Chaz.

"Hello?" I answered.

"Come over."

"But your date..." I began.

"It's over," he said. "Dinner was good, but I dropped her off and then came home."

"Be right there."

On the drive to his apartment, I kept going over our conversation. He had turned down sex with a near-stranger, in order to have sex with me. This was not his modus operandi. In fact, it was something I couldn't quite comprehend. Was he falling for me? I couldn't tell. But I also suddenly knew that I was more than just sex. This—me and him—it was real. I was real to him. And that was all I needed to know.

Valentine's Day was a few days away, and while I'd never had a real boyfriend on the actual holiday, I found myself for the first time with a reason to celebrate. It was nothing particularly romantic. In fact, I drank Midori Sours while he pounded Guinness, and then we watched a couple movies before passing out. But it was ours, and it might have been the best Valentine's Day I've ever had.

"You make me feel awkward but amazing," he'd told me that night.

In the course of our time together, I began learning things about him, things I never thought I'd be privy to. Although he came across as the "I-don't-give-a-fuck" guy, there was more routine ingrained in him than I'd realized. He had a way of doing things that I was certain not to infringe upon, although I found it amusing. He struggled with insomnia, so I'd fall asleep hours before him, knowing full well that by 4 or 5 a.m., he'd join me. He never was much of a cuddler, but there was always that part of him—usually his neck up against my back or a stray foot across my calf—that had to be touching me.

As for the sex, it was a constant. When we were apart, we sent one another suggestive text messages, and emailed naked pictures back and forth, both things I never thought I would do. And once together, we had sex multiple times a day, and it was always exciting and new. Sometimes in bed, sometimes on the couch. Now and then he'd pick me up and, legs straddling him, carry me over against the wall and pound away until both of us would collapse in exhaustion. At night, we'd fuck on his balcony, protected by the shadow of the outside tree, yet turned on and fueled by the fact that any passer-by could hear us. He was the only person—up until and since that point—who could make me orgasm from sex alone. It was like his touch was heroin, and I, a junkie who craved it, couldn't function without it.

February moved quickly, and before I knew it, it was my 21st birthday. A handful of my closest friends showed up at the local sushi restaurant and bar for drinks, and Chaz played sugar daddy to me, buying me an assortment of alcohol-laden fruity-sounding beverages—Sour Patch Kid, Long Island Iced Tea, Fish Bowl, Pineapple Paradise—until I was good and liquored up. After I drank more than my fair share, ensuring a rough day to follow, my friends left and he took me back to his place, where he made me pizza and forced me to drink water. There was gratuitous birthday sex involved, and we finally fell asleep as the sun was coming up. In spite of my horrific hangover, I'd never felt so well taken care of.

At some point—and I'm not quite certain when or how—our connection became a relationship. We weren't just co-workers sleeping together; we were two people practically living together. And this evolution prevented the strained uncertainty that taking the next step in a real relationship involves. There was no hesitation over how certain actions might be construed or misconstrued. I wore his socks to bed because he had spare ones and knew that my feet always got cold. I stocked his refrigerator with my grocery essentials because I ate half my dinners there. I left my toothbrush in his bathroom because it didn't make sense to always tote it with me. And one day in mid-March, as we sat in the living room, him flipping through a magazine and me reading a book, he turned to me suddenly.

"Let's move in together!"

"Uh. What?" I asked.

"Let's be roommates," he said. "It makes sense. You practically live here anyway. I'm looking for a bigger place. There's no one I'd rather live with. We're great together. What do you say?"

"Yeah," I said nodding. "We are pretty compatible. I'll think about it."

But I was scared to think about it. Things were so perfect and so right between us that I was afraid thinking about them or attempting to mess with them might change us. We were at a level other couples only ever dreamed of being at, but we hadn't even tried to get there. We just were.

And so that's why, when I met someone new a month later, I left Chaz.

The two weren't even comparable. This new guy was cute but Chaz was hot. He was smart but Chaz was brilliant. He was funny but Chaz was hilarious. He had a job but Chaz had a career. He was good in bed but Chaz was a stallion.

But there was one area that he had Chaz beat. He was so enamored of me that he wanted me to be his girlfriend. And while Chaz and I had never had the relationship talk—it had never been necessary—I figured deep down that if he'd really wanted to be with me, he would have asked me to be his girlfriend.

So one Monday in April, after my first date with the new guy, I told Chaz about him.

"I think I just want to be friends," I said.

"OK," Chaz said, not demanding an explanation. "But if you change your mind, I'll be around."

"I know," I responded, knowing that I wouldn't change my mind.

It wasn't that I wanted to leave Chaz. In fact, he was the greatest lover I'd ever had, and maybe ever would have. But it was something else. I'd managed to get that far without falling for Chaz. But I knew, deep down that was exactly what was happening. And if I didn't cut if off first, I knew that he'd be the one to break my heart.

So instead, I ended things, preferring to walk away from the table intact as opposed to risking losing everything. It was a safe move at the time—I didn't yet know, that I'd later refer to him as the one who got away. And then I'd only have myself to blame.

DAVEY

It was October when I spent the evening in San Francisco with Dave. It began as a no-expectations kind of thing. We were both burnt out on flighty friends. His had all moved to other cities hundreds of miles away. Mine were still around, typically only when things were convenient for them. The loneliness of his situation was overtaking him, while the fair-weathered nature of mine left me feeling somewhat desperate. It made sense then, that we sought one another's solace.

At first, I wasn't sure what to think of him. He was in his 30s, and had come from Alaska to California nearly a decade ago, seeking to escape the oppressive and lonely life up north. The winters of his childhood in Anchorage were especially cold and the daylight was limited half of the year. One day, when he was 23, he left home. He impulsively decided upon San Francisco; where he spent his first summer, couch surfing on the edge of homelessness.

An animal rights activist, Dave was a reformed-vegan, now a vegetarian. This was before I, too, immersed myself in the animal rights movement, so I was intrigued. He worked at a local non-profit animal shelter, in charge of the cats. It was a no-kill shelter, but he confided in me that sometimes they had to put cats down anyway; it was considered the less cruel option to euthanize the ones that were brought in too sick to be healed. I could tell as he talked that it broke his heart, and this was part of what appealed to me. I'd encountered plenty of people who took up causes to boost their image, and I knew that Dave was someone special because he had a genuine vocation. It gave him a sense of purpose that I'd found lacking in so many others. His empathetic nature made me think that he could be the exception in the string of boys who had treated me badly.

Although I hardly knew him, for me, his way of living was semi-exotic. He was a little bit too reckless, but I liked how he made me feel uncomfortable. I was not fully at ease the short time I spent with him, at least not initially, although whether it was because he was more experienced in the life-game or because he had no intention of slowing down, I wasn't certain. He listened to dirty street punk and hardcore, smoked too much and rode bicycles. On paper, there was nothing to not like, although I'd always been a cynic so I had had my doubts.

Our evening rendezvous took place at a nondescript cavernous room of a bar that was entirely empty except for the two of us. He had worked all day, whereas it was already my weekend, which gave me plenty of room to fret over and change my outfit a handful of times and spend the hour-long drive into San Francisco worrying about how our time spent together would turn out, especially considering that it wasn't a real date.

I drove through Upper Haight in search of a parking spot, my least favorite activity magnified by the hustle and bustle of the weekend. A familiar tense feeling came over me as I turned down side streets, slowing down at driveways that disguised themselves as probable parking spots and sighing at pedestrian tourists who walked into the street at four-way stops just as I was about to accelerate.

It was then that he called me. As I myself was an avid text message-r, the fact that he called instead of responding with a text caught me off guard, but I had to answer.

"Hello?" I said tentatively.

"Hey," he responded. "Where are you?"

"I'm here, looking for parking."

"Cool! I just got off work and have to ride my bike home still. It will probably be another 30 minutes," he explained. "I live on Grove Street. Want to just hang out in the area and I'll call you when I'm ready?"

"Sounds good."

"See you then."

Thirty minutes seemed like a good amount of time to pull myself together and calm my nerves. But finding a parking spot took up the greater part of that half hour, and as I finally made it on foot to the corner of Divisadero and Grove, a few blocks from where I'd parked, my phone rang again. I looked down. It was Dave.

"Hey, I'm on the corner," I answered.

"Be right out," he said.

I looked up the street, scanning both sides, curious to see which house he'd come out of. Within a matter of moments, I saw him step out onto the sidewalk. He saw me, smiled, and began walking toward me. And next thing I knew, we were walking into this dimly-lit establishment and awkwardly making small talk over the shitty reggae music playing loudly through the sound system. He bought me a drink, and we sat down on barstools. The bartender lingered within earshot, and after shooting Dave an ill-at-ease look, he suggested we move some place more private. We promptly relocated to a back corner.

As Dave talked, I studied him. He was slightly taller than me, although only by an inch or two, and had soft, light freckles, which I'd not noticed before. In true biker fashion, his right pant leg was rolled up, and he hadn't bothered to put it back down. His hair was black—though he told me it was actually a natural reddish-brown, and that he'd been dyeing it for years. He spoke both hurriedly and quietly, in a voice that demanded I pay close attention. While he started out sitting up against the hard wooden booth, he eventually relaxed and gradually leaned in toward me, his posture growing slack. And it was then I realized that while I'd found myself feeling anxious before we met up, I was now overcome with a different kind of anxiety—I didn't want our time together to end. After thirty minutes or so, we finished our beers and decided to migrate somewhere less void of ambiance, or at least some place with a better music selection.

It was dark outside when we set out down Divisadero Street. He took me a few blocks down to The Page, but it was already crowded with people. Instead, we crossed the street and backtracked, settling on the Mojo, a hybrid bike shop and café that was nestled back from the street, difficult to spot unless one was specifically looking for it.

We sat in that little place, which was just around the corner from his apartment, for hours it seemed, leaning over a small table lit by a candle, sharing our stories of defeat and triumph, of family and friends, discussing favorite bands and albums. But what got me the most was how he remembered things I'd told him. He asked me questions and really wanted to know the answers. He got excited but apologized for interrupting me or going on tangents.

Although he hadn't indicated that he liked me, I detected that certainly uncertain feeling, the one where sometimes you just know to keep going. I took a deep breath.

"There's another thing about me," I began.

He looked back inquisitively, but let me continue.

"I just went through a bad breakup. My ex left me a few months ago. I thought we were going to be together forever, but he thought differently. I'm not completely over it, so I thought I should be honest. That's what I'm going through right now."

He nodded slowly, and then spoke up.

"I went through a bad break-up a couple years ago," he said. "I know it's not the same, but I kind of get where you're at."

"I'm just a little emotionally damaged," I added.

"You have to be, to experience heartbreak," he said. "We're all a little emotionally damaged."

Then he told me about his family.

"My mother is blind," he began. "I still feel guilty for leaving her behind. But my sisters...they're more successful than me, more ambitious than me and I know they love me, but I don't think I'll ever earn their approval. They think I'm irresponsible."

It was refreshing, to let someone in and in turn be let in. Perhaps I shouldn't have been so trusting, but I could feel myself growing fond of him, and my reservations moved aside.

By this point, "hanging out" had clearly evolved, and by beer number three, I was pretty sure we were onto "kind of being on a date." I made certain to keep things on an even ground by purchasing every other round, still wary and unwilling to give him the upper hand. Occasionally, when he'd stand up to use the restroom or order the next round, I'd sneak a peak at my phone, sending texts to a friend to let her know that Dave had received a green light.

After drinks, there was a tentative moment where neither of us said a word, as we both seemed to be feeling out the other person's stance. It only lasted for a second, and I didn't suggest anything; I just followed him as he put his arm around me and guided me around the corner, walking far too knowingly in the direction of his apartment. Up the stairs, quietly, and through the front door, where he warned me to watch out because his cat might flee. Then we went into the kitchen, where we cracked open a bottle of Fernet-Branca and poured ambitious shots into mugs. I had a water back and he had a Sierra Nevada.

We sat down at a round table in his kitchen, which looked out into a courtyard in the center of the building. Our conversation settled on names. Middle names, married names, maiden names.

"Most people call me Dave, although I get David sometimes," he told me. "Though you can only call me Davey if you're sleeping with me."

"So I'll be calling you Davey by morning then," I shot back.

He looked up from his beer, but said nothing.

I poured another round of Fernet and we toasted one another before gulping them down. I set my mug on the table as he stood up to smoke outside. Standing behind me, cigarette dangling out of his mouth, he stopped short and turned around. Grabbing the cigarette from his mouth and resting it on his ear, he placed his hands on my shoulders and started massaging them and my back. Slowly, tentatively, he slid down into the chair behind me, running his hands down my sides. Then he gently took his hand and placed it on the side of my face, and with the slightest movement of his palm, shifted my head to the right until I was nearly facing him.

"You're gorgeous," he began. "Can I kiss you?"

He never gave me a chance to answer.

His cigarette fell to the ground, forgotten, as we drunkenly stumbled through the hallway, tripping over our eagerness and spilling into the walls, kissing hard and anything but furtively. We went through the doorway into his room and he pushed me down onto the bed, falling on top of me, but not before he slammed the door shut behind him with his foot. He didn't tremble or miss a beat, and there was no fumbling as he reached around and under my shirt to unhook my bra. In spite of being massively inebriated, he knew what he was doing.

Yet, unfortunately for both of us, Dave had drunk so much that he had "whiskey dick." The result—produced by the Fernet and not whiskey—was that Dave could get it up but not keep it up. In spite of this setback, we still haphazardly attempted to have sex, although it never resulted in much of anything aside from us collapsing into laughter and starting the cycle all over.

After several more endeavors, we both lost our enthusiasm and drunkenness gave way to sleepiness. Although the window was open and the nearby ocean breeze chilled the air, I slept soundly and warmly, with Dave's hand in mine, his legs wrapped around my legs, his head nuzzled into the nape of my neck. And when the sunlight began to shine in through the window, he moved in closer and snuggled tighter.

It was nearing 10 a.m. when Dave finally began to stir, and as I rolled over to face him, he smiled and kissed me.

"Good morning Davey," I said slowly.

Without a word he began taking off our clothes, until once again, we were naked. But this time, we were sober, and the connection was intense. He looked in my eyes as he entered me again, whispering dirty talk to me. Yet the sex still managed to retain fragments of awkwardness, left over from the night before. He slipped out of me more than once, and I smiled patiently each time, reaching down with my hand to guide him back inside me. When we finished, he fell down next to me, and we promptly fell asleep again.

Eventually it was time to get moving. He had to work, although he was already considerably late. I had errands to attend to, so we got dressed. But as I put on my clothes from the night before and he picked out an outfit for the day awaiting him, he threw on some vinyl. I had told him the night before that I liked the band This Bike Is A Pipe Bomb and he had asked if I liked This Is My Fist. When I said I hadn't heard them, he assured me that they were worth checking out. And now, the morning after, he made good on his promise of playing them for me. As he pulled on his pants and buttoned his shirt, he danced around his room, singing along with the songs. I sat on the edge of the bed, wiping the sleep from my eyes, enjoying both the music and the show taking place in front of me.

"I could get used to this," I thought to myself, as I stood up and slipped into my jeans.

After we were dressed and ready, we headed out the door.

"I have to run to the corner store to buy cat food for Freddy," Dave said. "So I'll just walk with you."

We traveled the three blocks to my car together, and as we approached it, he stopped and kissed me. I retrieved my keys from my bag and he asked me to call him when I was in town again. I told him I had every intention.

So of course I made him a mix—one for drunken nights and tangled limbs, followed by cold San Francisco mornings in bed.

FORGET YOUR TAUGHT TALKING AND LESSENING LESSONS

Indictment – **Jawbreaker**
I Drink the Wine – **The Murder City Devils**
High Tide in Alaska – **Native Nod**
We Invent You – **Unwound**
Song for Friends to Me – **Faraquet**
Sleepin' Around – **Sonic Youth**
We Will Not – **Paint It Black**
A Simple Gesture – **J Church**
That's When I Reach for My Revolver – **Mission Of Burma**
Middle of the Night – **American Steel**
Basil's Kite – **Cap'n Jazz**
This is the Part We Laugh About – **Medications**
Pause – **Kid Dynamite**
Circles – **Dag Nasty**
Ordinary Life – **Samiam**
Almost Ready – **Dinosaur Jr.**
Holy Wars – **The New Trust**
Tight Frame Loose Frame – **Smart Went Crazy**

In the days that followed, I did my best not to contact Dave, although he was all I could think about. I knew I was coming from a pessimistic sort of place, the result of heartbreak that made trusting another person unappealing. Yet Dave had inspired a minute amount of hope inside of me that made me think maybe there were guys out there who weren't total jerks, guys I could be in a relationship with after all. And I was sucker for the way his rough exterior gave way to a sensitive core. Though we had only shared that one night together, I felt like our intimacy progressed beyond that. Still, I didn't want to blow it, and I knew that seemingly clingy and obsessive girls could do just that.

After a few days I finally texted him to let him know that I would be in town the following weekend. No response. Realizing he was the type who preferred phone calls, I called and left a message. Again, no response. I decided not to contact him until the day of. The morning I set out for San Francisco, I texted him again, but with a very casual message, stating that if he wanted to get a drink, I would be around. I was hoping to imply no strings, because, after all, one night of promiscuity doesn't constitute a relationship. He finally texted back and said he'd be around, and for me to contact him when I was free.

I went about my afternoon with friends until dusk, when we parted ways. It was at this time that I called Dave. Again, no answer. Admittedly, I was nervous. Things had gone so well the first time around, and his standoffishness began to make me worry. I left a message saying that I was in town, and decided to grab a bite to eat to kill time. After more than an hour had passed and I still hadn't heard from him, I realized I'd been stood up. So I gave up and drove home.

In the weeks that followed, I attempted to contact Dave once or twice more, but eventually came to the realization that—for whatever reason and in spite of whatever connection I thought we'd made—I'd essentially been reduced to the equivalent of a one-night stand. It was disheartening, not because I had an issue with one-night stands, but because I thought we had connected on a deeper level. And maybe we did. But in his mind, I wasn't worth pursuing any more than that, and I would never know the reason why.

Yet I still had a mix, albeit an impotent one, and while I didn't necessarily need to have the last word, I wanted him to have it, because I made it with his enjoyment in mind. So one evening when I knew he wouldn't be around, I stopped off at his work and delivered it to him via a co-worker. I don't know if it ever got to him, and if it did, whether he even listened to it or not, but I could finally be at peace with the fact that I unabashedly put myself out there with no regrets. And slowly but surely, Dave began to fade from my mind.

Then, nearly three months later, we had a chance encounter. It was New Year's Eve. I had started dating someone new a couple weeks after the Dave incident because, after all, the best way to get over someone seemed to be to get under someone else. And so I was surprised, and astounded, and completely taken aback, when I arrived at the Hemlock Tavern with my friends for drinks and a show and saw him there. In some kind of cruel, serendipitous twist of fate, This Bike Is A Pipe Bomb was playing, and as I stood on the edge of the crowd of punks jumping around to the music, taking in the very last song of their set, Dave passed in front of me. We made eye contact, but he didn't show any signs of recognizing me. It was only an instant, but I knew without a doubt that it was Dave.

Shaking, I exited the room and approached my friends. Of the group, only one, Leigh, was familiar with the situation, so I ran it by her quickly.

"Remember Dave?" I said.

"Yeah, so," she replied, seemingly disinterested.

"He's here. Like, *here* here. I just saw him by the band."

"*What?*" she inquired, now engrossed.

"He's here. What do I do?"

"Well," she began. "Do you like him still?"

"Huh? Um, well. Not really. I mean, I got over him, but I want to know what happened."

"Then go talk to him," she replied. "Be the bigger person. Say hello. You won't come across as desperate. I'll be right here if you need me."

I set down my pint glass, quickly pulled myself together, and made my way across the bar to where Dave and his friends were congregated.

"Hey there," I said, tapping him lightly on the shoulder. He turned around to face me, and I continued. "Dave, how are you?"

"You don't even know me!" was the harsh reply. I stood, looking him in the eyes, an expression of shock plastered across my face. His reaction seemed to come from nowhere, his words making little sense in my mind. If he hadn't meant to answer me in such a cold and senseless way, he gave no indication of it. I had no idea how to respond, and before I could, he had turned to his friends, his back facing me once again.

My heart began racing. I couldn't tell if his friends had observed what had happened, but regardless, I suddenly felt so insignificant. A loud burst of laughter came out from the group, and it didn't matter what they were talking about because I was certain it was about me. The punch line of a joke I didn't even understand. All I could think about was how badly I wanted to cry. No one in the entire bar was looking at me, yet I felt as though everyone was.

And then, just as quickly as the humiliation took over, it was gone, and in its place was anger. How could I let someone make me feel so vulnerable? How could he just treat me like a total stranger? I wanted to tap him on the shoulder again and punch him in the face, but I knew better. It wasn't that I wanted to hurt him, but I just wanted him to recognize that he had hurt me.

I began walking across the bar in a bit of a daze.

"How'd it go?" asked my friend.

"He didn't want to talk," I replied.

She looked at me, confusion spread across her face, but then everywhere around us, people began counting down from ten.

It was almost the New Year, and as the room chanted in unison, "THREE, TWO, ONEEEE!!!!!" everyone around me erupted into cheers and screams. As for me, I pounded my beer, slammed it down on the table and left the bar. There was nothing else for me to do.

ETHER

It was a rainy night in February, just after Valentine's Day, a holiday I'd always managed to be indifferent about. I was sitting on the couch in the living room of our three-bedroom house in Petaluma, wrapped in layers of clothing and blankets, because we never used the heat in that house.

"We're heading to the Hemlock," my roommate Leigh said, motioning to a friend standing nearby. "Wanna come?"

"Yeah, come on!" Anne chimed in.

"Naw, I'm good here," I told them, glancing up from my computer screen. "I'm just going to write."

Leigh and Anne exchanged glances, and then looked at me. Leigh shrugged.

"Bammer dude," she said, her slang word for something that was disappointing. "Come on out if you change your mind."

Leigh went back in the bathroom to finish applying her makeup while Anne lingered in the hallway. She emerged a few minutes later, her otherwise quiet entrance betrayed by the loud clacking of her boots against the tile. She grabbed her purse and looked back at me, offering up one more plea. I smiled and told them to have a good night.

With our other roommate out of town for his birthday, I had the house to myself. After deciding to make myself a late dinner, I relocated to the kitchen, bringing my laptop with me and placing it on the table.

As I began rummaging through cupboards and refrigerator drawers, I heard a familiar noise from my computer—my inbox had an incoming message. I shuffled across the floor and saw that it was another email from Ether.

He and I had been writing short emails to one another for close to a week. Having recently been laid-off from my reporting job, I had a lot of free time, in addition to the surplus of loneliness I'd been feeling for months. He was a punk rocker living in the Bay Area, and naturally I latched onto him as a friend after replying to a posting he'd made online about punk rock. It wasn't just the companionship I was after. I was well aware, if only on a subconscious level, that the way I related to boys was through music. And so that's exactly what we talked about, with the main topic being the upcoming Zero Boys show at Gilman Street.

But on this particular evening, Ether wanted to do more than talk about music. He wanted to meet up. I sighed, knowing our relationship was on the brink of evolving from totally safe and mostly anonymous, to, well, something else. The thought both excited and scared me, but after a few back-and-forth messages in which I resisted while he insisted, I finally gave in.

"Meet me at the Hemlock in one hour," I said, opting to get together at the bar that my friends and I frequented.

I quickly changed out of my pajamas, stopping to send a text to Leigh and let her know that I would be joining them after all. Looking in the mirror, I laughed at how unkempt my hair was. To my right was my green beanie, which I hastily used to cover my head. Grabbing my keys and putting on a jacket, I headed out the door, running quickly to my car to avoid getting wet.

With the rain, the 40-minute drive to the city was slower going than I expected. I texted Ether to let him know I was running late and he told me not to worry, but I still drove faster than I should have.

It was nearing midnight as I made a U-Turn at the light on Van Ness Avenue and Polk Street. I turned down Hemlock Street; the small alley the bar was located on, and found parking immediately. I turned off the engine and texted Leigh and Ether both, to let them know I had arrived. Then I stepped out of my car, locked the doors, and began walking down the sloped alleyway toward the corner.

I was maybe 50 feet from the corner when I saw a figure standing in the rain, smiling, and looking up at me. It was Ether.

I breathed a sigh of relief, noting that he looked just like his pictures. He was taller than me, about 5'10", with kind eyes and a defiant edge to his smile.

"Hey," I said, as I walked closer.

"Hey," he said. "Let me buy you a drink."

He gestured toward the door and I led the way, stopping to pull my ID out of my back pocket and show it to the bouncer before stepping in.

As I entered, Leigh came running up to me.

"Is he here?!" she asked excitedly.

"Ether, Leigh. Leigh, Ether," I said, making the introductions.

She shook his hand as he glanced around, and then pointed to a corner of the bar.

"We're sitting over there, if you want to join us."

Leigh walked away and Ether turned to me.

"What are you drinking?"

"Newcastle."

"One Newcastle coming up. Go ahead and sit down. I'll come find you."

He turned to the bar and ordered a drink for each of us, and I made my way over to the group, where Leigh was gushing to Anne.

"He's cute," she said, before turning to me. "Good work."

"You guys," I said shyly. "It's not a date. We're hanging out. As friends."

"Doesn't look that way to me," Anne teased.

I was about to object but saw Ether heading in our direction so I quickly stopped talking. Since there were no chairs nearby, I suggested we sit at a table in the corner.

We sat down and started drinking and talking. He was from Sacramento, which is where I had gone to college. Coincidentally, for a short while, he had attended the same high school as my college best friend. When he was barely old enough, he joined the army to piss off his parents. After fighting in Afghanistan, he was discharged with an injury. Since then, he'd gone from living as a homeless veteran on the streets, to living with his mother back in Sacramento, to where he was now, in an apartment on Treasure Island.

The whole time he talked, Ether was tapping his foot along with the music playing from the jukebox, all of which was punk rock or indie. He would ask me questions, then stop mid-sentence to sing along with his favorite part of a song, returning again to what he was saying once it was over.

This went on for the next hour-and-a-half: talking, drinking, singing. With each beer he became slightly more boisterous, while I became slightly more enamored. Sneaking peeks at him, I noted his bleached blonde hair sticking out from underneath a pageboy hat, and I had to admit, his carefree attitude was contagious. Only hours before, I'd felt next-to-nothing for him. Now, I was beginning to fall.

When last call came around, he looked straight into my eyes and asked if I wanted to get something to eat. I agreed, but just then, Leigh and Anne approached me.

"We're heading home," they said. "Are you OK to drive, or do you need a ride?"

I could tell they were offering me an out, a safe way to escape the situation if things weren't going well.

"I'm fine," I said, letting them know with my eyes that things were more than good. "We're going to grab a bite together."

Leigh smiled.

"Have a good night then. And text me later." She turned to Ether. "It was good to meet you."

"You too," he said.

He picked up his pint glass and drank up the remaining liquid, and then we set out, walking a few blocks to the nearby Mel's Diner, where we sat and ate greasy food, in hopes it would soak up the alcohol.

After we finished eating, we lingered at the restaurant for half-an-hour to sober up. As the time neared 3 a.m., Ether grabbed the bill and went to pay for it. I wasn't tired. Ether wasn't either, so when he suggested we drive around aimlessly, it didn't strike me as odd. We walked back to my car and I drove down Polk Street, eventually intersecting with Market and heading toward the Embarcadero.

A mixtape from a friend was playing on the stereo and each time we hit a red light, Ether got silent, so all we could hear was the music. I knew that he was planning how he was going to make his move, but rather than throw him any indication that he was going to be successful, I relished the awkwardness building up to the first kiss, and I wondered when he would finally be brave enough to do it, if it would even be tonight.

"Let's go to Dolores Park!"

His words broke the silence of my thoughts and I shrugged.

"Sure, why not?"

I drove down Mission, making my way to the corner of Dolores and 18th, parking my car at the church the park was named for, Mission Dolores. We jaywalked across the street and over to the park. By this point, the rain had let up, but the ground was still soggy. Ether extended his hand, and I gripped it tightly as we treaded up a hill along the muddy grass. He led the way to a large metal container situated in the middle of the park and climbed up, reaching down to help pull me up. Once on top, we surveyed our view of an open field and empty streets running alongside the corners of the park. It was a rare moment, being the only ones in the park, because I was so accustomed to sunny afternoons where every square inch of space was filled with hipsters on bikes and punk rockers with dogs, everyone reading, or drinking out of brown bags, or waiting to be the next Craigslist Missed Connection.

My thoughts were interrupted when Ether lay down on the cold, wet metal, pulling me close to him.

"We didn't meet one another until the day after Valentine's Day," he said. "But can we still be one another's Valentines?"

It was at this point that he finally worked up the courage necessary to make a move. Yet when he kissed me, I found it wasn't like any other first kiss. Instead, I felt a spark run between us, jarring me. I nearly jumped, unprepared for the intensity of our initial physical connection, but dismissed it as nerves. We kissed a few more times, and each subsequent kiss felt like a jolt of electricity. This continued until the rain began again, lightly sprinkling down on us.

"Let's go back to my place," he said. "Don't worry, no sex. I just want to spend the night holding you."

I nodded in the darkness.

Ether jumped down to the ground, then stood behind me, his hands reaching up to my hips, to ensure I wouldn't slip and fall as I made my descent. He took my hand and once again led me, this time to the car. I turned the key in the ignition and drove, one hand on the wheel, one in his, as he gave me turn-by-turn directions to his place. We drove alongside the road that ran the perimeter of Treasure Island, and I remember looking out at the city glowing on our left and feeling euphoric.

When we arrived, he unlocked the door, then turned and put his finger to his lips, before slowly opening it. We walked in, and after he locked the door, all I could see were streaks of the street lights illuminating segments of him as he stopped to take off his boots. I followed, removing my own shoes. Then he started up the stairs, and I crept along behind him. At the top, he entered the first door on the right, waiting until I was inside and the door was closed before he turned on the light.

The room was plain, simple. There were posters on the wall—the Misfits, some Oi! band I'd never heard of, and Che Guevara. There was a desk in the corner, piled high with empty soda cans and Cup O Noodles, books and stacks of papers. In the corner was a mini fridge. Most notably there was no bed—just a pillow and a pile of blankets on the ground. The closet door lay open with clothes strewn about, and garbage was collected in a couple of piles. Yet the stark contrast of his living standard with my own didn't bother me—not then.

I sent a text message to Leigh, informing her I wouldn't be coming home that night, and then set my phone down, as Ether kissed me again. He turned off the light and the two of us got closer.

As I inhaled his scent, a sense of warmth took over. And then I felt it again: that raw, unfiltered connection. When he touched me, I felt like I was being shocked, and every time we made contact, a shot ran up my spine as chills spread over my arms and upper body. Contrary to our decision to not have sex, the clothes came off, and all I felt was heat, running through me like an electric current. I'd heard people talk about chemistry before, but I always assumed it was an overstatement. Yet with Ether, it felt real. We seemed to be physically bound together.

The sun woke us the next morning, but we paid it no mind, until just past noon. I sat up, stretching, while he still lay beside me. It was only then that I looked at my phone to see missed messages from Leigh, reminding me of our plans for the day.

"What are you doing baby?" Ether asked sleepily, reaching out with his right hand in an attempt to get me to lie down again. I grabbed it with my own and stroked his arm.

"Figuring out when I need to leave. I have to go up North, you know. I have plans."

"Bring me with you."

It was settled then.

We dressed and made our way off the island, stopping at a convenience store to get coffee and cigarettes. As we got onto the Bay Bridge heading East toward Oakland, Ether picked up a mixtape from the floor of my car and inserted it into the cassette deck, trading it out for the one from the night before. I heard the click and the hum of the tape player, and then it began.

The song "Son of a Gun" by the Vaselines was playing. A few minutes later it was over. Ether reached over and hit rewind, starting it from the beginning again.

We drove north to meet with friends for a tour of Lagunitas, a local brewery located down the street from the house I lived in. Forty-five minutes into the tour, our whole group was drunk, and it was there, sitting on the orange couch in the brewery tasting room, that Ether asked me to be his girlfriend. This was a request to which I drunkenly and wholeheartedly replied yes. My logical side attempted to reason with me, but all I could think of was that chemistry, and how close I already felt to him. It had to mean something. And although I hadn't even known him for 24 hours, it felt right.

Once we were back at the house, Ether and I fell into bed and took a nap. We woke up an hour or two later, found some snacks in the cupboards to tide us over, watched a movie, and drank some more.

It was at this point, drunk off homemade screwdrivers, that Ether confided in me three important parts of who he was. He had Post-Traumatic Stress Disorder from the war. But his PTSD was compounded by the fact that his little sister had killed herself when she was in high school. Both of these things led him to drink, and he told me that night, sitting on the edge of my bed, head in hands, crying, something he'd been afraid to admit to me before.

"I'm an alcoholic," he said.

I hugged him and let him cry. After some time had passed, I spoke up.

"Ether," I began. "I don't care. I will do whatever you need me to do to support you in this, even if it means not drinking."

He looked up at me and paused.

"You don't have to do that," he said.

"But I want to. You don't have to feel so alone. I care about you."

In the week that followed, we spent the majority of our time together playing house, sleeping, eating, talking, fucking. We replaced alcohol as a vice with sex instead, and strangely, it was how we best communicated. Whereas sex had always been mostly inconsequential in my previous relationships, with Ether it was how we grew to know one another. And we trusted one another. I knew just what to do to get him to cum: a finger up his asshole, my mouth sucking his nipple—things that once seemed repulsive or kinky to me were now completely commonplace and even erotic.

And the chemistry, it was still there. When Ether touched me, I got distracted, lost in him. I felt as though I couldn't exist without him. Unfortunately, the chemistry happened to be the only thing that we had going for us, although we had no way of realizing that then.

Since my car only played cassettes, and since we spent so much time in it, driving back and forth from the city, and since we were sick of listening to the same ones over and over, I decided to make a mixtape for Ether. I took a cue from The Vaselines' song—which was "our" song—opting for a mixture of sweet, indie-pop and twee-inspired songs.

I WANT TO SEE YOU WHEN THE SUN GOES UP

Son of a Gun – **The Vaselines**
You and Me – **Tiger Trap**
Fucking Boyfriend – **The Bird And The Bee**
Just Because of You – **Sambassadeur**
Parentheses – **The Blow**
Secret Nothing – **Cub**
Funeral Face – **Suburban Kids with Biblical Names**
Sunshine Soul – **The Gerbils**
Ever Fallen in Love (Buzzcocks) – **Nouvelle Vague**
Loveseat – **The Softies**
Space Manatee – **Heavenly**
Every Day – **Voxtrot**
Ticking Timebomb – **All Girl Summer Fun Band**
What's Important – **Beat Happening**
Sweet – **Tullycraft**
Modern Mystery – **Someone Still Loves You Boris
Yeltsin**
Biskitt – **Psapp**
Stars – **Au Revoir Simone**
I Just Do – **Go Sailor**
Boats and Birds – **Gregory ₵ The Hawk**

The songs I picked seemed to express a longing for something lasting, something which would break my established pattern of dead-end relationships. But in spite of what the carnal nature of relationship might have indicated, we also seemed to fight a lot in that first week we were together. Deep down, I knew it wasn't healthy, what I was doing, but for the first time in my life, I'd been presented with something physical that was so undeniably alive and real, and I didn't want to let it go, not without seeing where it might lead.

The fights themselves were always a combination of my stubbornness and his uncontrollable rage. We butted heads over the most insignificant of things, and while we wrestled one another to solve most of the disagreements, playfully fighting it out, once a day, one or two problems would slip through the cracks, evolving into something bigger. More often than not, it would end with me crying, and him trying to console me, and then the two of us having sex.

One afternoon, in the week after he'd stopped drinking again, I was in the garage sorting through laundry when Ether came up from behind.

"So who do you like more, drunk Ether or sober Ether?" he asked, putting his arms around me.

I paused.

"Sober Ether," I replied. "Drunk Ether is...a bit overkill."

The truth was, drunken Ether was too clingy and love-struck, especially after such a short amount of time together. But he was also overwhelmingly sweet, something the sober version could have stood to take notes on.

It was sometime in early March when I was driving Ether to the city, and we got in another stupid fight. This time, he was mad that I hadn't dropped him off at the corner of Octavia, like he wanted. I was annoyed because he hadn't communicated to me where he wanted to be let off, other than "in the Haight."

I came to a stop at a corner and he angrily unbuckled his seatbelt. Without questioning my plans for the day, he got out of the car and didn't say a word as he walked away.

I sighed, frustrated, and turned right off Masonic Avenue and onto Waller Street, first parking, and then walking a couple blocks to meet up with my friend. Air lived just down the street, on the corner of Haight and Clayton. He owned a record label, which he operated out of his home, so I knew I could stop by anytime I was in the neighborhood and he was likely to be around.

"He sounds like he's punk as *fuck*," Air said sarcastically, when I told him about the tumultuous relationship with Ether, all of which had transpired in the short time since we'd last hung out.

"He's had a rough time," I said, making excuses. "I see a lot of potential in him, and physically we totally work, but..."

I trailed off.

Just then the phone rang. It was Leigh, who was also in town.

"I just parked in front of Air's house."

"Come on in!"

I walked to the front door to let her in, and we made our way back to Air's bedroom.

"We're going shopping. Want to join us?"

Air looked at his computer, then back at us.

"I've got a lot of work to do, but let's have dinner later?"

"Alright, we'll call you in a bit."

As we walked down the steps and rounded the corner, we saw Francisco making his way toward us. He had bussed over, knowing I was in the neighborhood.

Francisco was sarcastic and incredibly vain, but rightfully so, for he was one of the most beautiful boys I'd ever met. He took pride in his toned physique, styled hair and poster-boy smile. He sported a two-day shadow and his eyes always glinted mischievously. Since he knew how attractive he was, it was probably the only reason he got away with such sass.

We stood on the sidewalk, outside American Apparel, while Leigh searched inside for deep-v shirts in her favorite colors. Francisco, meanwhile, was telling me about his new beau when, in my peripheral, I saw someone looking at me intently. As I turned to face him, I realized it was Ether.

My face immediately lit up and I rushed to hug him, no longer annoyed with the attitude he'd copped earlier. He was wearing his cheap black sunglasses that he loved, but didn't bother to take them off.

"What the hell are you doing here?" he questioned, half-curious, half-accusatory. "I didn't know you'd be sticking around in the city."

"You didn't ask," I thought, but kept it to myself.

"This is Francisco," I said, introducing him to my companion.

"I'm Ether."

He extended his hand to shake, but his raised eyebrows directed themselves toward me, as if to question what *I* was doing on *his* turf.

Ether then introduced me to his friend, and I asked his plans for the evening, which the friend answered for him. Ether was only half-listening now, tooling around with his cell phone, like he did when he was either bored or not interested. I took it as a sign to wrap up the conversation and part ways.

Ether walked off, suggesting I call him later. I agreed, although I knew he probably wouldn't answer. He was weird like that, choosing unpredictably when to respond or not. It bothered me slightly, but I didn't care enough anymore to make it an issue.

"Who was *that*?" Francisco mouthed at me, as Ether walked off.

"The boy," I responded.

"He looks homeless."

The words came out, forceful and full of disdain. Francisco's non-verbal communication said everything I needed to know about his first impressions, but I didn't try to defend Ether this time. I knew that beneath the layer of snark, Francisco was merely looking out for my best interests.

Taking Francisco's comments into consideration, I decided Ether and I had seen too much of one another in recent days, so I avoided contacting him for a few more. I didn't hear from him either. Eventually, after I decided enough time had passed, I sent him a text message.

No response.

I sent him an email.

No response.

I called him and left a message.

No response.

I had been through this before with other boys, the one-night stands of my past, but I figured Ether owed me more. Yes, we'd only been together a few weeks. But I was his girlfriend. I was entitled to hear from him every once in awhile, even if it was just a message to let me know he was OK.

After a day of fretting and worrying, I received a message from Ether via a social networking site.

"Stop calling me," it read. "I don't want to talk to you and I don't have to."

I was shocked. Completely floored. I called up Leigh immediately.

"I think Ether just broke up with me through an internet message!"

"What a d-bag," she responded, suggesting we have a girls night out to help me forget about it.

The next couple weeks were filled with multiple girls' nights out, which in turn were filled with far too many vodka tonics, as I tried to shake Ether from my mind. It took every bit of self-control I took to resist contacting him, and I wanted to smash the mixtapes in my car that reminded me of him, or perform some similar dramatic gesture to make myself feel better, but I didn't, instead taking things one day at a time.

So I was surprised when he texted me one evening with a song lyric. I was out in the Mission, hanging out with a group of friends on the back patio at El Rio, crowded under heat lamps. Air and I were sitting at a table, completely stoned, after eating cookies his roommate had made. Leigh was flirting with a boy, and Anne was sitting between Air and me, begrudgingly taking in the whole scene.

I texted Ether back with the next line in the song, and this went on for a few hours. Whether it was because I was high, or because I knew he'd eventually contact me again, I wasn't sure, but nothing felt out of place.

The next day, the cycle began again. I drove back to the city, picked him up and drove him back to his place.

"I was scared," he said, holding my hand as I drove on the Bay Bridge, back toward the island. "I like you. Way too much. And I don't know how to deal with you, because you're real."

I took in his words, thinking that they were sweet, all the while attempting to dismiss how rehearsed and fraudulent they felt.

He turned to me suddenly as I took the left exit onto the island.

"Let's get married!"

"Uhhhhh."

"Let's do it. Let's just run away. To Humboldt. Let's live up there together. We don't need anyone or anything."

I smiled at his impulsiveness, his carelessness, and instead said nothing. For as much as I felt that connection with him again, I could already sense the bipolar nature of our relationship. Of course he was saying this now, but what would he be saying in a few hours, a few days?

And while my mind was telling me to run, my body went into override mode, telling me that I was back where I needed to be. While I hadn't felt the need to be with him when we were apart, the moment we were in the proximity of one another, it started up all over again.

Yet, just as I predicted, a week or two later, we ended up fighting, and I didn't hear from him again. This time I didn't bother contacting him, because I knew it wouldn't matter.

Nearly a month went by. I got accepted into graduate school, moved to another house, and started sleeping with someone new. Ether wasn't around for any of those things. And this time, instead of being ignored by him, I was also the one ignoring him—by refusing to chase him. I decided I could be as immature and stubborn as him, knowing that he would cave in if I didn't.

And eventually he did.

It was toward the end of April when I received a text from Ether. It was out of the blue, except for the fact that I knew it would arrive someday. I just didn't know when.

His text messages was, per usual, a song lyric of sorts, something about fighting, or war. I didn't recognize it so I texted him back.

"What are we even fighting about?"

"I don't even know anymore."

And then my phone rang.

I was in the bathtub and it was late, so I didn't answer. The call went to voicemail, and moments later my phone buzzed with another text.

"If you don't answer, I can't talk to you."

I highlighted his name and hit "Send."

He picked up the phone on the first ring and I remained silent, waiting for him to talk first. It was strange, and somehow natural, to hear his voice. We talked about our respective days and I filled him in on the new changes in my life. I spoke in hushed tones and an unwavering voice, trying not to give away anything that I was feeling.

He asked me if I was happy.

"I think so," I said.

I told him about Zeke, the boy I had started dating, and as he replied, I could suddenly hear tension in his voice.

"Is he your boyfriend?"

"No. Just someone I'm seeing. He's a great guy, but I don't really feel anything for him."

Our idle chat continued a few more minutes, but all the while, I sensed he hadn't called me to catch up.

Finally he got to the point of the entire phone call, and as he spoke, I could hear the smile in his voice.

"Get your ass down here," he said, playfully yet forcefully.

"Give me a couple hours," I replied.

I paused.

"Leigh's going to be so mad at me," I sighed.

"I really don't like that girl. She's a bitch."

"Don't worry, she hates you too."

And just like that, we were back together again. It seemed more normal than the first two incarnations of our relationship. I didn't let his quirks or rants bother me as much as they used to. Our interactions were also more on my terms, and I made it clear to him that he certainly wasn't my boyfriend.

On a Thursday night, the last day of April, I drove down to spend the night with Ether. It was a week after we had started dating for the third time, and the day before his birthday. I arrived late and brought a chicken burrito with me, made just the way he liked it.

He opened the door and kissed me quickly, grabbing the food from my hands. We headed up to his room and sat down, where he immediately turned his attention to his laptop, unwrapping the foil from the burrito. Without a word, he began eating, and continued reading what he was involved in before. And suddenly I felt like I wasn't there. I ate my food in silence. When we were both done, I looked at him earnestly and he kissed me.

"Are you going to fuck me now?" I asked him.

We hadn't had sex since we started seeing one another again the week prior. It felt off to me.

He smiled half-heartedly.

"It's late. I'm tired, baby."

He turned out the light and lay down.

I thought he was joking, but quickly realized he wasn't. I was annoyed—mostly because he had made a valid point. It *was* late. So I curled up beside him and before long, sleep took over.

But as quickly as it came, it disappeared. I woke with a start. Panic set in immediately, but it took a moment to register why I was suddenly so afraid.

I saw Ether sitting up, talking to himself frantically. He smacked the palm of his hand against his skull, over and over and over, and I could hear the dull thud of skin and bones against skin and bones. He stood up and flicked on the light. He paced the room, mumbling. The volume increased, an urgency entered his speech, and suddenly he began yelling, screaming at himself. I knew he had night terrors, but wasn't prepared to encounter one.

He turned to me and began yelling at me. He told me that the images wouldn't go away. He closed his eyes and described how he saw nothing but death. His mind never stopped. His brain was always going going going. Somehow this was my fault, because I couldn't make it stop. I couldn't fix him. Uncertain, I put my arms around him to comfort him.

"Don't fucking touch me," he screamed.

He pushed me, hard.

I began crying, silently. But then it hit me. I shouldn't have been afraid of the person I was with. I deserved better. I looked him directly in the eyes, resolute.

"I'm leaving."

He stopped cold. Like a cliché deer in the headlights, he stared at me, unable to move, unable to speak.

Suddenly, he began to unravel.

"No, no, no, no...," he said.

I could see the certainty with which I spoke scared him. He was no longer in his night terror, but very much aware of what was going on.

"I'm sorry baby," he began, the tension leaving his face. "Come here baby."

I had been sitting in the middle of his room, my shoe in hand, looking around the room for my clothes and the rest of my belongings. I was frantic and afraid and trembling hard, refusing to believe I'd let it progress so far.

"Come here," he repeated, reaching out with his arms and pulling me to him.

I was hesitant but didn't resist, and gave no emotional reaction as he wrapped himself around me.

"I'm sorry, I'm sorry, I'm sorry," he repeated, rocking me. "Please stay with me, just stay with me."

He begged me over and over with desperation in his voice. I was still crying and it felt all too familiar to me, but instead of comfort, all I could think was that I couldn't subject myself to Ether's cycle any longer.

We lay down next to one another and I thought that he didn't want to fall asleep because of what his dreams might bring him, and because he might wake up to an empty room. But suddenly he calmed and before long, his breathing settled into a regular pattern. My cheeks were still wet from the tears and I remained wide-awake, turning my options over and over in my head. I stayed the night because I was afraid of what would happen if I left. But I couldn't sleep because I was afraid of how he might hurt me if I did.

Eventually my heart stopped racing. I let my eyes close and allowed the feelings of fear to fade away. Before long it was morning again, May the first. He was 24 years old and I had seen him through the night. But now it had become time for me to move on.

"I need to go," I told him.

He begged me to stay a few minutes longer, just a few minutes longer, and I lay down next to his warm body and held him. It made me feel safe, but I knew better. I knew I had to leave then or else I never would.

I ran my fingers through his hair and caressed his ear.

"Happy birthday," I said, kissing him gently on the forehead.

I stood and stepped into the hallway, closing the door lightly behind me. I slowly made my way down the creaky stairs and out the front door, across the lawn to the street and into my car.

I started the engine, rolled down the windows, and headed for the bridge. I didn't look in my rearview mirror, because there was nothing to look back on. It was the end. I knew it for real this time, and I think he knew it too.

ZEKE

"Wait, so you're a double major?"

I paused, cocking my head and shooting an inquisitive glance at Zeke, who was sitting a few feet away.

"I've told you this before," Zeke said, pretending to be annoyed with me for having forgotten.

"Don't tell me," I said, holding up a finger in his direction and stopping for a moment to think. "Oh wait! I remember. You're majoring in English and... Anthropology!"

Zeke looked at me with surprise.

"Wow! You're like an elephant. A retarded elephant."

Now it was my turn to look surprised.

"I get it. I get it. It's because I remember everything, but just not right away."

"Exactly."

If I hadn't known Zeke prior to then, I might have been offended, but I was used to his backhanded compliments, so I dismissed it. His wit was an acquired taste, but I could appreciate it from time to time.

It was April. Ether and I were on one of our breaks, and Zeke and I had been dating for close to a month, although dating wasn't exactly the best word for it. Hooking up was more like it, even if he did buy me lunch once. I even resorted to breaking vegan edge and eating cheese on that "date," because in spite of knowing I was veg, he was firmly set on going out for New York-style pizza prior to spending the afternoon people-watching in Golden Gate Park. There was also our obligatory first date, which consisted of him buying me drinks at Toronado, a bar in the Haight that specialized in specialty brews. But whether he paid that night because he was making up for being late (which I later learned would be routine) or because he wanted to get lucky at the end of the night, I wasn't entirely sure.

Neither of us was too serious about the other, which is likely why occasional antagonizing and complete frankness characterized the entirety of our six-week relationship. The whole time, both of us were also dating other people, something that I'd long been accustomed to, but which Zeke was still attempting to get a grasp on.

"I don't understand dating in San Francisco," he said. "It seems like no one wants to commit. They all just want to fuck each other."

"And what's so wrong with that?" I asked.

"I just feel like no one believes in love anymore."

That was another thing about Zeke— he desperately wanted a girlfriend. And while I juggled a handful of males that I was only remotely interested in, Zeke was—at the time—only seeing me and one other person. The other, an exotic-sounding girl named Carmel, was his idea of girlfriend material. She, on the other hand, was looking for something more akin to what Zeke and I had.

It was easy to see, from an outsider's perspective, that he was looking for a love connection in all of the wrong places, but that didn't stop him from trying. Ever the romantic, he was always working to attach meaning where it didn't exist, and while it was cute to see someone who still believed in the notion of conventional romance, I thought he was slightly too idealistic.

Not to mention, most everything about Zeke was hyperbolic, starting with the way that he talked and trickling down into every facet of his life, all the way to how he wrote, which is how he expressed himself best. Whereas social situations often left Zeke indiscriminately saying things before thinking them through completely, his writing was solidly constructed and effectively executed. On an intellectual level, he was one of the only people I dated who I ever felt was on a relatively similar plane.

Zeke was also the first—and last—writer I ever dated. Other boys I'd been with wrote as hobbies, or by trade. But he wrote for the same reasons I did: deep down inside, every inch of his being propelled him toward verbal expression. It was his way of communicating with and understanding the world around him. I immediately recognized this in him and felt a conflicting affinity; I was drawn to him because he was a writer—and I was repelled by him because he was a writer.

Our time together was highly sexual, yet completely unromantic. His bluntness came as a welcome relief, and I never once had to initiate physical intimacy. In that sense, Zeke made me feel like I fit the gender norms, and I gladly allowed him to call the shots in bed. He had the tendency to be offensive in his stereotyping, but I never felt like I emasculated him. Not surprisingly, he never got me off, but he never tried to either, and I didn't make it an issue.

He did endeavor to keep me satisfied with the occasional foray into dirty talk territory, a turn-on for me, which I encouraged him to at least try out. But even those attempts somehow managed to be clumsy and ineffective.

"Do you have a tight pussy?" he asked me, seductively whispering in my ear the first night we were together.

"Yeah, I do," I replied. "It's tight and wet and ready for you."

Later on, after sex, he turned to me.

"Your pussy is OK," he said. "But I've had tighter."

That was my first real exposure to his potential for cruelness, but I was too drunk to do more than look at him in shock, my mouth agape. And after several more experiences dealing with his frequent word vomit, I began to realize that he wasn't someone ridden with bad intentions; unfortunately, he just didn't have much of a filter.

The initial reason I had zeroed in on Zeke as a conquest was superficial; his looks were more than vaguely reminiscent of someone else I knew. The two weren't anything alike in personality, but both were lanky white boys with Jewish noses and brilliant blue eyes—close enough in my mind. I had already blown my chances with his quasi doppelgänger, so Zeke started out serving as the Kim Novak to my Jimmy Stewart, a la "Vertigo." I was aware that this semi-psychological displacement was completely calculated and slightly fucked up, but I didn't care, not then.

And I was filler for Zeke too. I never knew what function I served in his life—if it was purely sexual or if there was something emotional going on as well. I suspected that I was only supposed to be a one-time venture, a stop along the route toward navigating the sexual state that characterized relationships for 20-somethings in San Francisco. But something about me had resonated with him, and I don't know if he ever was able to isolate what exactly it was. Since neither of us ever desired or even considered a real relationship with one another, I think he realized I was a safe bet.

"I'm not like every other girl," I'd told him, when we first started sleeping together.

"I doubt it," he'd replied. "That's what every girl says."

He had a track record of relationships gone awry with girls he'd never hear from again. By his telling of the story, most of them turned out to be completely crazy. Meanwhile, I still talked to most of my exes, even if only once every couple of years, a fact I pointed to as proof of my normality. That's the exchange he got for being with someone with whom there were no romantic feelings—sex was just sex. I also grew to genuinely care about him as a person, and as a result I could give him honest feedback on girl problems, especially since I was never once jealous of his affections for other women. In a way, I could fill both gender roles for him. I functioned as a female in our sexual relationship by fulfilling his sexual needs—unapologetically making out with him and giving him mind-blowing head whenever he was horny. And I functioned as a male in our platonic friendship, hearing him out and giving him advice, and never shying away from any topic of conversation. In that sense, he realized I was right: I *wasn't* like every other girl.

The sex was fun but I could have gone without it. It was our interactions afterward that I most looked forward to. He always wrote before he went to sleep, so I would stay in his bed—a double mattress on the floor, pushed up against the right angle where two of his bedroom walls met one another. He would get out of bed and put on some clothes—in the evening it was always a white undershirt with plaid flannel pajama bottoms. Sometimes I'd lay naked, eyes closed, making half-asleep conversation with him as he typed. Other times I'd throw on a T-shirt and sit up against the wall and randomly choose a book from his bookshelf to read. Always when he went to bed, he set the timer on his laptop to play music for a certain amount of time. Usually the mixes were folksy indie crossover-to-mainstream bands like Bon Iver or Iron & Wine. And unlike when I spent the night with a boy I *really* liked and couldn't fall asleep, I never experienced that problem with Zeke.

Zeke was peculiar in his taste. He reminded me of someone who shopped at Urban Outfitters, listening to music and reading books that held some kind of pop cultural significance. He dressed clean cut, usually sporting a plain T-shirt or baseball tee, with jeans, his outfit made complete by Vans or Converse and a zip-up hoodie. He was always quick to label himself as "not a hipster" and make fun of those who were, even though they tended to share many attributes. His nickname for me was "Mipster," short for "Metal Hipster," because of my snakebite piercings and tattoos. Perhaps it was meant to be delightfully offensive, but I thought it amusing more than anything else, and graciously accepted it.

That was another thing about Zeke: he was always coming up with nicknames for everyone. For instance, my roommate Leigh, the demanding, high-maintenance, boy destroyer who always got her way, was JAP—a Jewish American Princess. And he felt he could call her that, he said, because he was Jewish too.

Most of the time, his sarcastic approach to life was something I liked about him, but occasionally, his flippant attitude bothered me. In particular, I never felt much at ease when he questioned why I garnered so much male attention. It was clear that I got much more play than him, but I'd always attributed this to my personality—I was charismatic in my interactions with the opposite sex, and so the fact that I was always seen by men as the cute one as opposed to the hot one never bothered me until Zeke brought it up. There were infrequent jabs at the issue of my looks, particularly my weight. Without him having to mention it, I was already painfully aware of the fact that I wasn't his "type." I'd seen pictures of girls he dated or lusted after, and they were all unrealistically skinny, waifish hipster models. I was probably the first girl he'd dated who weighed more than him, and it hurt my feelings that he could so easily go from appreciating my breasts for their size to carelessly insulting me because I wasn't 115 pounds. There seemed to be some kind of disconnect between his expectations and reality and I wanted to break things down further for him, but it seemed pointless. Instead, I did my best to ignore these disparaging remarks. When it came down to it, he was somewhat clueless about how to get on a woman's good side, and I don't think he realized the gravity of his words on the person he directed them toward.

Plus, he served as a good sounding board for my relationship woes.

"He sounds likes a dick," was his typical response whenever I would bring up Ether. This minor act of sticking up for me seemed to absolve him of past offenses, and I was glad when his line of thinking validated my own.

Eventually, our relationship ran its course. But where all past relationships come to a point of conflict, there was no catalyst for our ending. Zeke and I continued seeing one another until it no longer made sense; there was no sexual chemistry, and we were both far too self-absorbed to be of much use to one another. There was also little conversation over it, as we came to that gradual realization that we were just friends. Or maybe it was that in the course of our explorations, we became friends. Whatever it was, we remained on good terms, our interactions exactly the same, minus the sex. We continued texting one another occasionally, meeting up for lunch once or twice a month. I still stopped by his house in Ingleside every so often, where we'd spend the evening watching a movie or talking and drinking. We still slept in the same bed, but nothing happened and it wasn't awkward at any point.

It was then, when we were just friends, that I made him a mixtape. Oddly enough, the theme was of songs about love versus songs about lust, something he'd suggested. As an effective means of comparing and contrasting, I decided to use each artist twice, first with a love song and then with a lust song. The result was something remarkably similar to his own struggle of rationalizing love and lust, with the embodiment of our own relationship falling somewhere in between.

THE THIN LINE BETWEEN LOVE AND LUST

Marching Bands of Manhattan – **Death Cab For Cutie**

After the Movies – **Cursive**

Lucky You – **The National**

First Day of My Life – **Bright Eyes**

Girl Inform Me – **The Shins**

Red Right Ankle – **The Decemberists**

Heart – **Stars**

Luckiest Woman in the World – **The New Trust**

We Looked Like Giants – **Death Cab For Cutie**

From The Hips – **Cursive**

Available – **The National**

Lover I Don't Have to Love – **Bright Eyes**

The Celibate Life – **The Shins**

Everything I Try to Do, Nothing Seems to Turn Out Right – **The Decemberists**

Midnight Coward – **Stars**

Get Vulnerable – **The New Trust**

MARQUES

"Wanna bang"

I looked up from my phone and burst into a fit of laughter.

"You won't believe the text message I just got," I said, waving my cell phone in the air.

"What does it say?" asked Mandy, making her way from the kitchen to the living room.

"It's from Marques. He sent this message, out of nowhere. All it says is 'wanna bang'—there isn't even a question mark."

"Marques? Which one is he?"

"Oh, I don't know," I said, attempting to figure out how to explain him. "He's like, the random hook-up type."

"I guessed as much, you know, based on his message and all. But seriously, who talks like that?"

I laughed and set the phone down, choosing for the moment to ignore him, and instead walked into the kitchen, peeking my head into the refrigerator in search of a beer.

It was a Friday night and our group of graduate school ladies had gathered at Mandy's house to get ready for an evening on the town. It was late October and she had just turned 29, so in proper fashion, we wanted the end of her 20s to be celebrated in style. The plan was to walk downtown and do a bar crawl, which in a town of about 60,000 residents, meant hitting up the half-a-dozen or so bars located on or near the main drag. Afterward, we'd stumble drunkenly back to her house and crash out on various couches and assorted air mattresses throughout the apartment.

I was wearing my brand-new knee-high rubber, fuck-me black rain boots. I was always an accessory-based person, with relatively simple outfits that revolved around one main piece. My cohorts, however, fell more on the girly end of the spectrum, always taking care to have sexy hair, flawless makeup and cleavage-revealing shirts. While they huddled in the bathroom, double-checking their appearances, I milled around, nursing my now-open bottle of amber ale, and decided to put on some music. Since we were planning on going out drinking, I figured the Far East Movement's latest radio hit, "Like a G6," was appropriate both in style and lyrical content.

Thinking again of the unanswered text message, I sighed. Marques and I had a long and semi-exhaustive, circular kind of past. He was a relatively reliable booty call, but not too dependable in any other department, as I learned after only a short amount of knowing him. I'd once tried to date him, back when we first started hooking up, and found that he didn't want to commit. Or rather, he didn't want to commit to me. But he seemed to have no problem calling me up on a whim—or in this case, sending me unsolicited text messages—with only one thing in mind: sex. A younger version of myself might have taken offense to this, but I knew that I wasn't at a place in my life to be girlfriend material, and the fact that he'd consider calling me for sex alone was more of a compliment.

Marques first began as my post-Davey exploit. We were the same age and lived in the same town, and so it made logistical sense. The first time we hooked up was a weekend morning in my old apartment in Petaluma. The night before, I was out at San Francisco bars with friends. Excessive drunkenness had resulted in courageousness, or brazenness, depending on your point of view, and our text correspondence went from friendly to seductive in a short period of time. Marques was a straight-shooter when it came to telling me what he wanted, and instead of indulging my coy game of text message come-ons, he responded by calling me up, asking if he could come over that night. I told him I was out with friends but would call him when I got home. And I stayed true to my word, but he didn't answer my 3 a.m. phone call. Frustrated, I left a message and went to sleep.

The next morning, I woke around 10 a.m. to a phone call from Marques.

"What are you doing?" he asked in a chipper voice.

"Sleeping."

"Can I come over now?"

"Um. OK."

"See you soon."

He hung up and I sat in bed, slightly dumbfounded.

"This could be interesting," I said, to no one in particular.

Luckily, my roommate was gone for the weekend, so that was one less thing to worry about. But hooking up? On a Saturday morning? I wasn't even slightly drunk, and I wracked my brain for a reason to drink enough to get halfway to buzzed before he arrived, but my logic fell short.

It didn't matter, because Marques arrived a few minutes later and I had to let him in. We walked into my bedroom and I sat down on my bed. He took a seat next to me, and suddenly, I found myself feeling unnaturally shy. I was still in my pajamas— short shorts and an oversized shirt, absolutely no makeup, with my hair messily pulled back. But none of that mattered to Marques, who immediately leaned in and kissed me.

Pushing me down gently, he got on top of me, and began undressing us both, alternating between the two of us—first his shirt, then mine. When we were both naked, he stopped and stared down at me, smiling. The light from the bedroom window flooded in, glinting across his baby blue eyes and causing his entire outline above me to glow.

The sex was more tender than I expected, with him stopping every few minutes to ask if I was OK, if what he was doing felt good, if he should speed up or slow down. This attention to detail was something I later grew to love about him. I was self-sufficient, with a tough exterior, but Marques was always careful. He made me feel fragile, delicate, and feminine.

When we were done, we both got dressed, and not knowing exactly how to proceed, I offered him a drink. We walked into the kitchen and I opened the cupboard for a glass, which I then filled with water from the Brita. He took a few sips and then, setting the glass down on the counter, put his arms around me, rocking me back and forth and singing.

"You're too cute, blue eyes," I said, bestowing him with a pet name that would end up sticking.

He didn't say a word, and instead began kissing me again, on my cheek, on my forehead, on my nose. At the same time, he took his hand and slowly slid it down my stomach, into my underwear, his fingers pushing up inside me. I moaned slightly, leaning against the counter, and he wasted no time taking off his pants and putting himself back inside me, stopping only for a moment to put on another condom. It was quick this time, and as he came, I couldn't help but laugh to myself at the thought that every time I was cooking food, or unpacking groceries, or washing dishes from then on out, I'd think of what also went on in the kitchen, one Saturday morning in the Fall.

In the weeks that followed, Marques was slightly evasive, but I didn't mind. I was going through a big move, halfway across town, into a three-bedroom house. Shortly after I moved, I called him up and he said he'd come by.

"Hey you," he said as he walked in for the first time. "You know, you live right down the street from my work."

"Really?"

"Yeah, I'm in that shopping center where the grocery store is."

"Wait, don't you deliver pizzas?"

"Yeah, I work at that pizza shop on the corner."

He stopped for a moment.

"Yo, don't laugh girl. I know their pizza sucks. But it pays the billssss." He unnecessarily emphasized the end of the word, dragging out the last consonant.

I called Marques blue eyes, but he always had nicknames for me that were cute, in a generic way. His standards were usually "girl" or "boo."

"Wut up girl" or "Hey boo" were customary text message greetings. I found them particularly endearing because they struck me as something a rapper or hip-hop musician might say. And Marques wasn't anything like that—in fact, he was maybe as far away from those scenes as a person could be, seeing as he was the singer in a metal band and the guitarist in a hardcore band. He always dressed in demonic-looking T-shirt of bands I'd never heard of, which I jokingly told him he'd have to cover up if I ever took him home to my parents.

The months that followed were riddled with random hook-ups. But eventually, an unsystematic pattern began emerging. There was never a guarantee that he would come over when he said he would. Often times he called me with the intention of stopping by later, but failed to follow through. I soon learned not to plan my evenings around him. But on nights that he did come over, it was almost always a given that he had worked earlier. Rather than make the post-midnight trek across town, it made more sense for him to come over to my house, a few blocks away, and spend the night and every once in awhile, he'd even surprise me with a pizza or breadsticks.

We never talked about the other people we were seeing, but it was assumed on both ends that we weren't the only ones. I knew that the girls he dated were semi-groupies of his bands. We were both 24, and from what I could gather, the girls who regularly threw themselves at him were typically 18 or 19. The age difference was probably what guarded me against becoming too jealous, because I knew from personal experience how desperate younger girls could be. After all, I was one, once. Additionally, I was seeing other people, so I knew there was no point in even pretending to be protective of my relationship with Marques.

Yet in spite of all this, a few months into seeing one another, it suddenly dawned on me that he was beginning to mean more to me than I'd originally planned. He had come over one night and driven me out into the country in his red Toyota Yaris, to his band's practice space. During the entire ride he'd forced me to listen to selections from his iPod, the stereo turned up too loud, playing all metal. I complained, but I secretly loved the thrill of it. When we arrived, he took me inside, showing me around. I sat down on one of the beat-up couches in the room, and he sat down next to me, reaching behind him between the couch and the wall, retrieving a mason jar.

"Wanna get high, boo?" he asked, unscrewing the lid, removing a sealed plastic bag of weed and waving it around.

"Naw, I'm good."

I realized then, sitting in an old barn-turned-practice-space, examining posters on the wall as Marques rolled a spliff, that this was him letting me in.

"I wish you'd play something for me," I said, but none of the instruments were there, except the drums.

"Remind me later," he said.

When we got back to my house, he made his way to my room and picked up my white Telecaster from the corner.

"How about a song now?" he asked.

"Wait, I want Leigh to hear this," I said.

I opened my bedroom door and knocked on the door opposite mine.

"Come in," I heard.

"Marques is gonna play guitar. Wanna hear?"

"Yeah, bring him in here."

The two of us walked into her room, closing the door behind to trap the heat, and Marques sat down on her bed, while I sat on the couch opposite. The two of us listened to him play riffs of well-known songs, in addition to some of his hardcore band's music. He kept looking up every minute or so and staring into my eyes, as if looking for approval or validation.

"Pretty impressive," I said when he was done.

It was getting late and I could tell Leigh was getting bored, so we said our goodnights and went back into my room.

We went to bed shortly after, but it was the first night we didn't have sex. Instead, we lay on our backs, talking.

"You know Marques," I said, taking a deep breath. "I'm really starting to like you. I didn't expect this."

He was quiet for a while.

"I like you too. I just. I don't know what I want."

"That's OK. I know we're on different levels. You want to keep this fun, and for some strange reason, I want more. I mean... I'm happy with where this is, but I wanted to be honest with you, and let you know that you're more than just casual fun to me. Do with that information what you will."

He turned to me and kissed me on the cheek.

"Aww boo, you're so sweet."

It was his turn to be honest. He told me about another girl he was dating. That he wanted to see where things would go with her, but that she was messing him up, jerking him around, telling him she wanted to be his girlfriend but then sleeping with someone else.

"Tell her how you feel about what she's doing to you," I told him.

"Yeah? You think so?"

"Yeah. Maybe she'll realize you're serious about her. Or maybe she won't. But at least you'll be able to figure it out. I've been unhappy long enough. And I know the only way to be happy is to go after it. So do what you need to do. Just be honest with me in the process."

"I will boo. Thanks for that advice. And by the way, your ex? Fuck him for what he did to you."

I smiled.

"Goodnight Marky-Mark."

"Night girl," he said, as he cuddled up close to me.

In the next week, I set out to make a mix for him, with compromise songs that we both liked. The purpose of the mix was two-fold: I wanted to have something that didn't make my ears bleed every time I drove with him, and I wanted him to have something that made him think of me.

CONFUSED AND EXHAUSTED WITH A HEALTHY FIX

Shirt – **Jawbreaker**

Never Heard of Corduroy – **None More Black**

Mean Streak – **American Steel**

Lights Out – **Orchid**

Idle Hands – **The Murder City Devils**

Could You Be the One? – **Hüsker Dü**

Sick-o-me – **The Descendents**

Do You Like Me – **Fugazi**

It's All Up to You – **Black Flag**

Sky – **Converge**

Fragile – **Wire**

Existence – **Hot Cross**

Transitions From Persona to Object – **Botch**

Angel – **Paint It Black**

Blind Date – **Refused**

I Love Hardcore Boys/I Love Boys Hardcore – **Limp Wrist**

Without Her – **Cro-mags**

Expectations – **Youth of Today**

But You Are Vast – **Crime In Stereo**

Our Adventures Incomplete – **Ampere**

For Marcus – **The Plot To Blow Up The Eiffel Tower**

"Does Minor Threat have any love songs, or are they all about straight edge and staying positive?" I asked Leigh as she walked into the room while I was making the mix.

She gave me an exasperated look.

"What's this for?" she asked.

"A crush mix for Marques."

"I knew it! You definitely make that awesome faggy face when you talk to him."

"Oh shut up," I snapped back, returning my attention to the music.

When I was done with it, I texted him to let him know I had a mix for him. He came over later that week with his own laptop and a few blank CDs in hand.

"I'm gonna make you mix CDs too!" he exclaimed.

We spent the rest of the evening sitting around the kitchen table, drinking tall cans of Tecate and listening to music. Marques would play a song or two by a band for me, and if I liked it, he'd put one of their songs on the mix. If I told him I didn't like it, he sometimes still put a song on anyway.

"Trust me, you'll like this one boo," he'd say.

At the end of the night, I had two 80-minute mixes of songs to listen to.

"Put them in your car, girrrrrl," Marques said, as he kissed me goodbye.

I didn't hear from him again, until much later. I found out, through a social networking site no less, that he started dating the girl he'd told me about earlier, the 19-year-old who was playing games with him. The news made me sad, but it didn't bother me as much as I thought it might. I had sort of expected it.

I also expected it when they broke up, less than six months later. I didn't tell him, but I'd had a suspicion it wouldn't last. He contacted me shortly after that, but I'd moved on emotionally, and in my mind. He had been reclassified as hook-up—not boyfriend—material.

There were a couple encounters—once every six months or so—in the time between then and the October night he texted me out of the blue, some two years after we'd first hooked up. And although I laughed it off when the text arrived, I knew I'd eventually respond to him.

"I'm downtown drinking," I wrote back a few hours later.

"Girl, I wanna see you," he said.

Before I knew it, I was in the front seat of his truck—which was idling in the Bank of America parking lot across the street from the bar where my friends were—making out.

"Come home with me girl."

"Didn't you just move back in with your parents?"

"It's cool. I'll sneak you in. We just have to be quiet."

Not one to turn down a potential adventure, I agreed.

"As long as you have me back at Mandy's house in the morning."

I texted the girls to let them know I wouldn't be rejoining them, and Marques and I drove back to his parents' house.

"Take off your boots," he said, as we approached the front door.

I removed them, then cautiously and quietly followed him inside and up the staircase, into the guestroom where he was living.

Setting my boots down and taking off my jacket, I looked around the room.

"I like the decorations," I said sarcastically, referring to the antique dresser and lamp, and the framed photo hanging above them, all things his mother had clearly chosen.

"Yeah, you like that?" he questioned, attempting to be seductive.

We got down to business, but it didn't do my memories justice. Whereas sex with Marques always seemed to last thirty minutes, sometimes an hour, he came within a few short minutes.

"Oh damn," he exclaimed, afterward.

"What was that?"

"Sorry, I got nervous. I thought I woke my parents."

I laughed at the inanity of it all and kissed him.

"It's fine."

I reached for my phone, which was resting on the windowsill above the headboard. It was nearly 4 a.m. I set the alarm for a few hours later, and then fell asleep.

When my alarm went off at 7 a.m., I nudged Marques gently.

"Hey, you should take me home."

"Naw naw, it's cool," he said, wrapping around me tighter.

"OK, if you say so."

An hour later I could hear his parents waking up, walking around the house. I began panicking in my head, but thought that if he figured it was acceptable, it wouldn't be a problem.

An hour after that, he finally woke up, and as he got dressed, I put my boots on and texted my friends to let them know I was on my way back.

Marques had left the bedroom and was starting down the stairs by the time I approached the doorway. His mother was down below, and sensing him in her peripheral, began talking to him. I slowly made my way out, to the top of the staircase, before she noticed me.

"Oh..." she said, trailing off, speechless.

"Good morning," I said, attempting to be as casual as possible, and introducing myself.

She smiled courteously and shot a look of half-surprise, half-alarm over at Marques.

"I'm just going to drive her home," he told her.

"We have a lot to talk about when you get home, mister."

"It was nice meeting you," I called as I walked out the door. And then, under my breath, "Not bad, for a walk of shame with the parentals."

Marques fired up the engine to his pick-up, and I jumped in the passenger side.

"I hope I didn't piss off your mom."

"What? Her? No, she's fine."

He looked at me mischievously, holding my eye contact for longer than normal. Then, turning back to his car, he put it in drive and set off toward downtown, with me giving him directions to Mandy's house.

As we pulled up in front, he put his truck in park in the middle of the street. A semi-awkward silence followed, as I considered how to say goodbye. I glanced at the front bedroom window over his shoulder, and I could see the bottom half of the blinds bent open more than normal, with two sets of eyes peeking through.

"Oh no, it's my friends," I sighed.

Marques turned to where I was looking and waved, and I reluctantly joined in. Excitedly, Mandy and Abby pulled the blinds up further and waved back.

"Oh God."

Marques laughed and gave me a high five.

"Call me," he said, as I got out of the car.

I walked up to the front door as he drove away, and Abby greeted me, flinging it open.

"How was *your* night?" she asked, raising her eyebrows suggestively.

"Oh God," I said again.

She just looked at me and laughed.

"Wanna bang?"

JOSEPH

It was a typical weekend night in late March, and I was downtown with several visiting friends, indulging in conversation over pitchers of beer. But after a few hours, we decided to part ways, as they headed out to nearby Forestville, where they were staying.

As I walked out of the bar, I glanced down at my phone. Even though it was almost midnight, I felt like the night wasn't over. I punched a few buttons and moments later my phone was ringing.

"Hello?" yelled the person on the other line. It was Cruise, a long-time acquaintance. We always announced our mutual intention to hang out every time we had a random run-in, but neither of us ever really followed through. In the background I could hear people talking and a television blaring, indicating some kind of bar atmosphere.

"Hey," I said loudly.

"Hello," he said again, this time a bit louder, in an attempt to drown out the noise.

"Are you downtown?" I asked.

"Yeah. Aleworks. Where are you?"

"I was at Russian River. Just left."

"COME OVER!"

I hung up the phone and smiled to myself. I'd always had a bit of a crush on Cruise and I think he knew it. Something had almost happened the summer we met, two years prior. We got high in a park after a party and he invited me over to spend the night. I was cautious and declined, opting to go home once I'd sobered up. I still get slightly mad at myself when I think about it, even though we both know it wouldn't have gone further beyond a night of inebriated making out.

At this point, I wasn't quite drunk, so I got in my car and drove the two blocks to where he was, parking across the street from the brewery. I walked in and quickly located him at the end of the bar. He was camped out with two friends, watching the hockey game; the Anaheim Ducks were his team. I gave him a hug and took a seat next to him on the barstool he'd saved for me.

"How ARE you?" I asked.

"I'm great," he replied. "So glad you called me!"

"Watching the game, huh?"

"Yeah," he said. "Go Ducks."

"Psh," I responded. "Go Sharks!"

He shook his head at me and smiled, making silent commentary, as if to say that I had given the most cliché answer he could imagine.

"Whatever," I said. "We'll see who makes it to the playoffs."

"Oh by the way," he interjected. "These are my friends, Joe and Jim."

He pointed to the two guys seated to the left of him, also engrossed in the game.

"Hey," I said, introducing myself, before turning back to Cruise.

We quickly became immersed in conversation. He too was a writer, and we talked about what we'd been working on lately and what books we'd been reading. Time passed quickly as we talked, and soon it was last call.

"I guess I should head home," I said, standing up.

"WHAAAAT?" Cruise exclaimed. "No. We're going to a party. Come with us."

"Where is this party?" I asked, as we exited the bar.

"Downtown, near the junior college," he said. "We're walking there if that's cool."

"Oh no," I said, agreeing in that moment to go. "I have my car. Let's drive. You guys want a ride?"

We all piled into my car and were on our way. Cruise sat in the front to give me directions, and five minutes later I was parking the car on Spencer Avenue, a tree-lined street in an older neighborhood in town.

The four of us got out of the car and followed Cruise's lead, as he made his way across the street and up the steps of a lit-up house. We entered the front room to the sounds of loud electronic music playing and a living room that was covered floor-to-ceiling in aluminum foil. I gathered from what other guests were wearing that the party was some kind of 80s-space-age-robot-themed deal, but no one seemed to mind or even notice that none of us were in costume.

As for me, I always seemed to know everyone in town, but after a quick scan of the room, I realized I didn't recognize a single person. Not one to be discouraged, I made my way to the kitchen where Cruise already was, talking with the friend who had invited him. Joe followed behind me, watching as I surveyed the drink situation.

"What *is* this?" I asked no one in particular, but Joe felt the need to respond.

"I know," he said tentatively, pushing up his glasses, which had slipped down his nose a bit, and looking around. "This is... *weird*."

I smiled, realizing I'd made a new friend.

"So, what's your story?" I asked as I picked up empty bottles of liquor, examining them for any untouched alcohol that might have remained at the bottom.

"My story?" he repeated, somewhat suspiciously. "Uh. Well. Um. I don't have one, I guess."

"Then how do you know Cruise?" I asked.

"Oh, you know, we're friends. We both spent a semester in England for school, I guess that's how we met."

"OK," I said, eyeing him skeptically. He seemed nice, but was a bit too timid for my taste. "I'm gonna scope out the scene."

I didn't ask him to follow, but he did anyway. I made my way to the nearest doorway and peeked inside. A bunch of

30-something ex-hipsters were all piled on the bed, dressed in shiny, new wave-inspired costumes.

"Who are YOUUUU?" asked an incredibly drunk girl from the corner of the room. I quickly introduced myself, noting aloud how weird it was that I didn't know a single person at the party, except the people I'd come with.

"You're cute," the girl replied. "I like you."

"Yeah, she's funnnnnnnny," slurred another.

I laughed, realizing I now had an attentive audience.

"Anyone want to hear a joke?" I asked.

Just then Joe looked at me with a questioning look in his eyes.

"You want to make yourself useful?" I questioned. "Go get me a drink."

He looked taken aback for a few seconds, but smiled. Obviously, the demanding female card worked well on him.

I turned my attention back to the room and began reciting my joke.

"So an octopus walks into a bar, carrying a set of bagpipes...."

Joe disappeared, and after I'd delivered my punch line, I continued talking to the people in the room, who were now playing a version of 20 questions with me. He returned a few minutes later with a plastic cup full of rum and Coke and handed it to me.

"Thanks," I said, smiling sweetly. "Wanna go out back?"

I didn't wait for his response and quickly left the room and headed down the hallway toward the back door, which was open. There were only a handful of people outside—the party smokers—so I sat down in a nearby lawn chair and Joe took a seat next to me.

Without the loudness, the intensity and all the people, Joe appeared more relaxed. I started asking him questions, and even though he was awkward, shy, and relatively insecure, I was intrigued. Certainly, he was not particularly memorable, but he was *nice*, and I rarely met nice guys.

I began a barrage of questions, to figure out as much as I could about him.

"Where are you from?" I asked.

"Atlanta."

"You don't have an accent."

"I guess not.

"Is your full name Joseph?"

"Yeah."

"Is it OK if I call you that instead?"

"Sure."

This continued for the next 20 minutes, until, after plenty of playful banter, we made plans to get breakfast together the next morning. We exchanged phone numbers, and then he suggested we try and find Cruise, who neither of us had seen for well over an hour.

We walked back into the house and searched the rooms with no sign of him.

"Maybe he's in the corner of the living room," Joe began, pointing to a group of people crowded around the DJ setup.

"Wanna make out?" I said, interrupting him.

Joe looked at me incredulously and I flashed him a devilish grin. I grabbed his hand, and without a word, walked toward the front door. He followed, and once we were outside, I led the way, around the corner of the house, down an alley, and against a fence, where I grabbed him and kissed him, hard.

We stood there this way, making out on the gravel path for five, maybe ten minutes. Then he stopped and looked around, suddenly aware of what exactly was going on.

"What if someone sees us?" He asked slightly paranoid.

"Who fucking cares?" I responded, grabbing his face and kissing him again.

"I mean, well, yeah," he said, glancing around again. "It's just. I've never really done this before. You know, made out with someone random. Like, I just got out of a long relationship a few months ago, and I haven't really, you know, been with anyone since."

"Do you want to stop?" I asked. "Cause we can stop if this is weirding you out or whatever."

"No," he said. "It's just. Yeah. No, I'm OK."

"Then shut up," I whispered in his ear, as I began to kiss down his jaw line, making my way back to his lips.

It seemed to do the trick.

Maybe thirty minutes later, we made our way back to the party.

"Where have you been?" Cruise asked. "I've been looking all over for you."

"We went on a walk," I quickly blurted out, knowing that given the opportunity to speak, Joe wouldn't be able to lie.

"We're going to another party," Cruise said. "Just down the street. Wanna go?"

"It's, like, 4 a.m.," I said. "I, for one, want to go home."

"Me too," said Joe.

"OK, whatever," Cruise responded. "I'll see you two later."

He headed down the street in the opposite direction. Joe and I walked to my car, and I started driving in the direction of his house. I pulled up outside and the two of us sat there making idle chat, until I leaned across and kissed him.

"Goodnight," I said. "Call me tomorrow? Maybe we can do lunch instead of breakfast?"

"Come inside," he replied, making his first bold move of the night.

He didn't need to tell me twice. I killed the car engine and followed him up the driveway as he warned me to be quiet. Slowly, he unlocked the front door, and the two of us made our way into the kitchen, where he offered me a cup of tea. I gladly accepted, and while we waited for the water to boil, I walked about the room, surveying all the details, from the dishes in the sink, the fruit on the counter and the magnets on the refrigerator.

"Those aren't mine," Joe said, following my gaze. "They're my roommate's."

"Who is your roommate?" I asked.

"This girl Christy," he said casually. "I think Cruise said you know her. You go to school with her or something."

"Holy. Fuck. Christy? Yeah, I know Christy," I said. Of course, of all the random guys to instigate a make-out session at a party with, I'd chosen the roommate of one of my classmates—of course.

My tea was ready, so I grabbed the mug and made my way into the living room, sitting down on the couch. Joe and I made small talk for a few minutes as I sipped the liquid. He was noticeably more relaxed in his own environment, but still appeared slightly anxious.

"Um listen," I said. "I better get home."

Instead of responding, he kissed me again.

"Well that was convincing," I said, setting down my mug on the wooden coffee table in front of us and leaning back on the couch. I kissed him again, and felt his hand on my hip. He began fumbling with the top button of my jeans, and I placed my hand on top of his and broke off the kiss.

"Not so fast," I said.

He looked at me with his head slightly cocked to the side, as if to ask what was wrong.

"Listen," I continued. "I like you. You're...different. It's refreshing. But seriously, I don't want to have sex with you. Not tonight. Because I know guys. I know that if I put out on the first night, you're going to say that you'll call me, but you never will. And maybe you want that, but I don't. If you want to have sex with me, I'm going to make you work for it."

That seemed to settle it. I fished around in my bag and found my cell phone, noting it was past 5 in the morning.

"I need to go home and sleeeeeeeeep," I said, drawing out my words to emphasize how tired I was. "Call me later today?"

He agreed and followed me outside, walking me to my car. As I opened the door, I gently kissed him before getting inside and driving off.

True to his word, Joe called me the next day, albeit relatively late.

"So much for that brunch," I said as I picked up the phone.

"Yeah, yeah," he said, dismissing it. "What are you doing?"

"Just finished homework. You?"

"Watching TV. Wanna come over?"

"Sure."

I made my way back across town to his place, and the two of us spent the evening camped out on his couch, watching OnDemand shows and getting to know one another. It went on like this—the conversation, the late-night hanging out— for another few days. He took me out to dinner at my favorite restaurant and played songs for me on his bass. We bonded over our love of Braid, Owen, and other Mid-Western emo musicians. We started a game of Words With Friends. We spent our time apart calling and texting one another. And of course, we made out a lot, but I never let him get too fresh with me.

Through all of this though, something seemed off. I kept telling myself it was just that he was so shy and unsure of himself. I admit that made me slightly uncomfortable. Living my recent adult life as the female aggressor in relationships was something I'd been trying to get away from. I was tired of feeling like I emasculated men, and I was tired of being the one doing all the work. I kept trying to push my doubts aside, though, because Joe seemed to have nothing wrong with him. He was relatively cute, and undeniably sweet, and I had been telling myself for some time that was what I needed in my life.

At the end of the week, I got a call from him.

"I have this movie that I need to watch," he said. "Want to watch it with me?"

"Sure," I said. "You want to come to my place? I've got the house to myself."

"Uh. Yeah," he said. "Um, wait, no. I'm kind of drunk."

"Want me to pick you up then?"

"Yeah. I'm at Cruise's house."

"Cool, I'll be there in 20."

I drove downtown and parked across the street from Cruise's house. I knocked on the door and Cruise's roommate answered.

"I'm here to get Joseph," I said.

He moved out of the way and gestured for me to come in. To my left, Joe was sitting on the couch, watching Cruise play X-Box.

"HEY!" he said jumping up excitedly.

"Don't stand in front of my game!" Cruise yelled.

Joe laughed dismissively and walked over to me.

"Ready to go?" I asked.

He grabbed his jacket and the two of us said goodbye, then walked to my car.

We got to my house and after a quick tour, went to my room and sat on my bed. I poured him a mixed drink and made one for myself. "How about that movie?" I asked, putting the DVD in my laptop.

We cuddled up close and started watching it, but the movie was wasted on us. Eventually I stopped it.

"Let's watch it later," I said, shutting my laptop down.

I turned out the light and snuggled up close to him, and we began to talk.

"What's the deal with your ex?" he asked.

So I told him the story of the big ex, the one who destroyed me. When I was done, he was silent, and we both lay there, staring up at the ceiling.

"I'm sorry," he said. "That sucks."

"Yeah, it did. But I'm better for it." I turned to face him. "What about you? What's your deal?"

"Oh, my ex. We broke up in November."

"Oh yeah? How long were you together."

"Six years."

"Shit," I said. "What happened?"

"I. We. Um. I don't really want to talk about it," he said.

"Um, OK. What was her name?"

"It doesn't matter."

I was silent and didn't push the issue, but secretly I was slightly hurt. It did matter. Not because I needed to know all the concrete details about this person. But I felt cheated. I'd just told him my story and been uncharacteristically vulnerable with him, and he gave me little in return.

It was quiet, and still for five minutes until I broke the silence of what we were both thinking.

"If we do this," I said. "Do you promise not to be a jerk after?"

"What do you mean?"

"I mean, sex changes things and I like spending time with you. Regardless of what 'all this' means, if after this happens, at some point, you decide that you just want to be friends, can you just have the courtesy to talk to me about it?"

"Of course," he said. "But it won't change things."

I felt reassured, but I also felt strange. Sex had never been an emotional issue for me—at least, not for a couple years. Not since the heartbreak. Maybe it was a purposeful kind of distance I placed on it. I knew alcohol had something to do with it. It was the only thing that made me feel normal enough to go through the motions of a physical relationship. But suddenly, I found myself weighing all the emotional implications involved in the sex act.

I quickly brushed those thoughts aside as he kissed me, and tried to focus on enjoying it. But I couldn't. Whether it was the fears running through my mind or the realization that the sex was a little too run-of-the-mill, I couldn't concentrate. After he came, he collapsed back onto the bed, and I cuddled up close to him, more out of routine than anything else. Still, I felt very far away—from him, from the moment, from everything.

I tried to let my mind go so I could doze off, when his phone rang. It was just past 5 a.m.

"Shit," he said, grabbing for it off the nightstand.

He answered the phone and had a quick conversation. Hanging up, he turned to me.

"That was Cruise's roommate. He has to go to work and my car is blocking his in the driveway."

I sighed.

"Let's go then."

I grabbed my keys and made my way outside to my car. We drove across town, with Joe apologizing the whole time.

When we arrived at Cruise's, he got out.

"I think I'm just going to crash here," he said. "I can sleep on the couch until I sober up."

I agreed and said goodbye, but there was no kiss from him. I assumed he was tired, and somewhat flustered.

I drove back home, suddenly somewhat angry at myself for having sex with Joe. It's not that I didn't want to beforehand. But I just felt so empty afterward.

After a short nap, I woke up and went about my day. I had a paper to write, so I set up camp in the garden, with a beer, my laptop, and a handful of books.

Joe called me in the afternoon.

"I'm home now," he said. "How's your day? How'd you sleep?"

We chatted for a bit and I asked him his plans for the night.

"I don't know, maybe hang out with Cruise."

"Well, call me if you want to hang out."

He never did call that evening. Actually, it was Cruise who called later, to invite me out with him and his friends.

I arrived at his house an hour later, and the five of us—me, Cruise, Joe, Shawn, and Jim—walked the half mile to a dive bar, where one of his friends was DJ-ing. During the whole walk, I talked with Cruise, since Joe was too busy acting weird and ignoring me. But it didn't surprise me.

Once at the bar, Joe continued to play the awkward card. So I did what I always did in situations like that: I drank more. And as I was standing by the bar waiting for my second or third vodka tonic, an older man approached me and started talking to me. He was creepy in that strange-old-man-hitting-on-a-younger-woman way, but struck me as relatively harmless, so I entertained his conversational attempts. All of a sudden I heard an unfamiliar voice on my left.

"Hey, you want to stand on the other side of me so this guy will leave you alone?"

I looked to see who had spoken—the guy next to me was about my age, and he smiled.

"Certainly," I said.

"Here, take a seat."

I sat down next to him and we got to talking.

"You a regular?"

"Yeah, I live pretty close by. Come here a lot. It's cheap."

"I've never been here before."

We progressed to talking about music.

"I'm in a hardcore band," he said. "Ever hear of Hoods? That's my old band."

"Wow. That's tight. We probably know a lot of the same people."

"Let's see!"

He grabbed my phone and started scrolling through the numbers, exclaiming every 10 or 20 names when he recognized a name.

"This is awesome," he said. "It's like we were fated to meet."

Our conversation extended until last call, and when I realized everyone was getting ready to exit the bar, I leaned in for a hug.

"Here, real quick," he said. "Give me your number. Here is mine."

As we were exchanging numbers, I glanced to my right and saw Joe standing a few feet away, talking with a loud and obnoxious girl in an Applebee's work outfit.

"Hey," he said loudly and uncertainly. "Can I like, have your number?"

She squealed something out and recited it to him. I rolled my eyes.

It wasn't until we were a few blocks away that Joe came up to me and put his arm around me.

"So who was that guy?" he asked defensively.

"Why the fuck do you care?" I shot back.

"Listen, you're not like, my girl or anything, but I just want to know."

"What, were you jealous?"

"What? NO."

"Who was that girl?" I asked, deflecting the question.

"She was just some girl. Whatever." He paused. "So, that guy..."

"I can talk to whoever I want," I said. "Besides, you ignored me all night. It's not like I had many other options."

I pulled away from his grasp and sped up, walking ahead of him. He had the common sense not to go after me.

When we got back to the house, Cruise offered me more to drink but I declined, asking for a glass of water instead. As I sat at his kitchen counter, Joe walked by, and grazed my knee with the tip of his fingers.

I was totally confused. After an evening spent being cold and closed-off, suddenly he was acting strangely intimate. It's almost as though he wanted his buddies to know that he'd sealed the deal—except he hadn't.

Suddenly my phone rang. It was the guy from the bar.

"I gotta go," I said, getting up to leave.

I said goodbye and Joe followed me out to my car.

"Who is that? Is that the guy from the bar?"

I laughed and gave him a small peck, then got in my car.

"Call me tomorrow, if you want."

The next day, Joe called me in the evening and invited me out for a drink at the British pub near his house.

We sat down at a table and started talking, and our conversation was normal again. It's like the night before had been a fluke. After he bought me a couple rounds, we decided to leave. But instead of walking back to his place, we took a detour alongside the creek.

Suddenly, he brought up the guy from the night before.

"What happened with him? Did you like him?"

"He was nice," I said. "But I like you."

"Um, but you got his number."

"He's the one who asked. Plus, you got that girl's number. Besides, if I didn't like *you*, would I do this?"

I leaned in and kissed him. Only instead of kissing back, he froze.

"OK," I said, breaking it off. "What's wrong?"

"Nothing. Nothing's wrong."

"No. Seriously. Your body language was *so* closed-off just now. What's up?"

He looked like he was trying to formulate words, but nothing came out.

"Let me guess," I said. "This whole thing...you...me...us. You're not into it anymore."

I watched as his face grew slightly fearful. He took a deep breath and then released it.

"Yeah. I kind of just want to be friends."

"I knew it!" I said. "You're a dick, you know that?"

"I'm sorry," he said.

"Remember when I told you to tell me if you weren't feeling it? That was bad form. But whatever, I'm cool just being friends. By the way, I fucked that guy last night."

"*What*?!" Joe said.

"I'm not your girl," I replied. "I can do whatever I want."

He laughed and seemed to visibly relax. I, meanwhile, feigned nonchalance, but deep down, I was hurt by him and angry with myself. He had turned out like all the rest.

In spite of the embarrassment of that rejection, we remained friends, spending a few evenings together each week. And it wasn't until perhaps a month later that I realized he was beginning to pull away again, which I found odd, considering our friendship had become entirely platonic.

He called me to apologize for flaking on our plans once again. He had made a specific point of wanting to meet for coffee and then drive me to school afterward. I thought it strange, but he insisted he wanted to see me, and that he would even drive me home after I was done with classes. I'd taken the bus downtown but when I arrived at the coffee shop, he wasn't there.

"Hey," he said when I picked up the phone.

"Where are you?"

"In Novato. I had to run some errands with someone."

"Ohhh?"

"Yeah. Um. This is probably weird. But I was with my ex-girlfriend. You don't think that's weird, do you? I mean, is it? It's weird, right?"

"Whatever. You hang out with whomever you want to hang out with."

"I guess. Sorry I missed coffee."

"It's cool. I have a bus to catch to school since my car isn't here. I gotta go."

I hung up before he could protest.

Only a couple weeks remained in the semester, and as it came time for me to focus on writing papers, I made a conscious effort to not talk to him. Yet in purposeful avoidance of him, I found that he wasn't making any effort to contact me. I figured at this point, he was once again involved with his ex, who both his friends and roommates had once described to me as "a controlling bitch."

In the first week of June, after school had ended, he finally called me.

"Aren't you leaving soon?"

"Yeah. Colorado in couple days. Then Europe until July."

"Oh. That sucks. I wanted to see you before you left. But I'm leaving tomorrow."

"Yeah? Where to?"

"A road trip. Going out to Atlanta to visit my mom. Also the East Coast to see some cousins. It's going to be about a month."

"Hmmmmmmmm," I said slowly, in a somewhat leading manner. "You're taking a road trip all by yourself? That sounds lonely."

"Well. Not exactly alone."

"Who are you going with?"

He paused.

"My ex-girlfriend."

"Sounds to me like she's a little bit more than that."

"*What*?! NO. No way. We're just friends."

"I call bullshit."

"No, really. We're friends."

I scoffed.

"You don't need to lie to me Joe. Whatever. Well, have fun."

"You too."

During the next couple of days, I received the occasional text message from him, letting me know what state he was in, what people he'd encountered, even what the hotels he was staying at were like. I thought this was strange, considering I still didn't even know the name of his ex-girlfriend, who he was traveling with. But after I flew to Europe, I heard nothing, and in the time I was gone, he didn't appear in my thoughts.

A month passed and I returned home, but not without a layover in the Atlanta airport. And a few days after I got home and had allowed myself to settle back into a routine, I decided to give him a call.

It went straight to voicemail.

"Hey Joe," I said. "It's me. I just wanted to call and check in. I was just in Atlanta; it made me think of you. How was your road trip? Let's get coffee and catch up. Bye." But surprisingly—or maybe not all that surprisingly—he didn't call me back.

A week passed. I noticed he had resigned from our Words With Friends game and deleted me from his social networks. It was more than disconcerting.

Unlike other boys I dated, I had never made Joe a mix. We simply weren't together long enough for it to have manifested, although the idea had crossed my mind. But now that we were apparently no longer on speaking terms, I began to re-imagine a mix—one with the same artists I'd have put on a "crush mix," but with much different lyrical intentions.

CLUELESS AS USUAL AND UNBELIEVABLY EASILY BRUISABLE

Thursday Side of The Street – **Knapsack**
Anyone Can Have a Good Time – **Owls**
Every Turn – **Hey Mercedes**
The Sad Waltzes of Pietro Crespi – **Owen**
I'm a Loner Dottie, A Rebel – **The Get Up Kids**
The Escape Engine – **Burning Airlines**
Pale New Dawn – **Jets To Brazil**
Consolation Prize Fighter – **Braid**
Get On the Floor – **The Promise Ring**
Revisionary – **Colossal**
Spit You Out – **Hot Rod Circuit**
Trials – **The City On Film**
Please Sleep – **Joan Of Arc**

Admittedly, constructing a list of songs by musicians he liked but with lyrics that weren't entirely positive was cathartic enough for me, although I knew he would never actually ever hear it.

I was telling my friend Jacky about this bizarre turn of events when I realized I was angry. Not because of what he did, but because of why. I'd wanted to know why.

I quickly shot a text message to Cruise.

"Is it just me, or is Joe acting weird? What is his deal? He won't even return my calls."

Less than 10 minutes later, Cruise replied.

"It's not just you," his text message read. "He has been a total asshole since he got engaged."

"What. The. Fuck."

"What's up?" Jacky asked.

I showed him the text message.

"That's fucked up!" he exclaimed.

"I know, right?!"

I held my phone in my hand for a few moments, deliberating what my next move should be.

"I just want to send him a text message. Something super passive-aggressive. Like, to let him know I know what's up. What should I say?"

"You want my advice? Don't send him a message. Fuck that guy. He's bad news and you're better off without him." I stopped and let the gravity of Jacky's words sink in.

"You know what? You're right. You're exactly right."

Without hesitation, I located Joe's contact information in my address book and hit delete. Instantly I felt vindicated.

I never talked to Joe again. I never even saw him. Months later at a concert I'd encounter my old classmate, who was now his former roommate.

"How's the new roommate working out?"

"She's awesome!" Christy exclaimed. "So much better than Joe. He's married now, you know?"

"Yeah. I assumed. Good riddance to bad rubbish?"

"Something like that."

I raised my Pilsner in the air, took a long cold sip, and smiled to myself.

OLIVER

"Natalye?" the email read. "Are you in love with me?"

I bit my lip and sighed. Of course he was on to me. But then again, that's exactly what I wanted him to think. And it wasn't far from the truth.

With little hesitation, I clicked on the reply button and hurriedly began typing out my reply, not bothering to read the rest of the email.

"Do I love you?" I began. "An uninhibited honest answer would be yes. What that translates to mean though, I can't definitively say. I'm not *in love* with you. I'm far too...un-capricious...to think or feel such a thing."

I paused, thinking about my word choice. No, un-capricious is not a real word, but the synonyms I could think of didn't quite express what I wanted to say. So my solution, which was based primarily on one thing (being drunk off Swedish boxed wine), was to find the best word to describe what I didn't mean, and make up an antonym for it. Un-capricious.

I laughed at myself, then glanced out the second-story window. It was dark, with only a single streetlight illuminating the neighborhood. Snow was falling across the strands of light, and I was struck with the feeling of being simultaneously poetic and ridiculous.

"Perhaps a better way of putting things: you make me feel infinite."

I stopped and reread the last paragraph.

"Good job," I told myself. "Way to quote *The Perks of Being a Wallflower* in your quest to be introspective."

Still, it would do. But I added a bit of clarification, for good measure.

"...with you, it's like a mind-fuck in a sense, where someone can get inside your brain, like you have mine, and made the synapses spark with excitement. I'm not confusing that for being in love with you, but I'm not going to sell it short either."

Satisfied, I hit Send, typed a few command-Qs to close the programs that were open, closed the silver lid of my laptop, and fell asleep.

It was January. Oliver and I had first gotten in touch in July of the year prior, beginning our Trans-Atlantic relationship. I cringe a bit on the inside when I think of how we met—through a dating website. Being somewhat of a serial womanizer, he had reached the age in his life where he wanted more than just a night with a stranger. He wanted to settle down and find someone to have a life with. Problem was, he didn't know how. At 36, he no longer considered himself a member of the bar scene, and the singles parties that *TIP* Magazine hosted on weekends in Berlin disgusted him. While beggars can't necessarily be choosers, he was the type who would pick spending an evening alone listening to a new record over a night out with what he referred to as "secretaries and 'smart' boys." So in his desire to find his dream woman, who excited him sexually *and* intellectually, Oliver turned to the Internet.

I had joined the website a couple years earlier. At the time, I was living with Leigh, who had undergone an intense heartbreak. The two of us bonded over our mutual disdain for love, or the idea of it, and in an effort to get back on the dating scene, we'd been persuaded by a few of our friends to try online dating. Given the generation we were a part of and the technology-laden world we'd grown up in, I viewed it as a perfectly acceptable and legitimate means of meeting a potential significant other. Still, after a couple of disappointments with people who appeared much more interesting on paper than in real life, I resigned myself to the fact the online dating was not for me. So I deleted my account.

A year later, Leigh and I were planning a trip to Europe, and in an attempt to make potential new contacts, I opened a new account. Although the website promoted networking that ranged from simple friendships to sexual relationships to long-term dating, I found that the few times I contacted females, they didn't respond, as friendship wasn't what they were looking for. So naturally the contacts I made were of the particularly good-looking, age-appropriate, and male kind.

Interestingly enough, I didn't first send Oliver a message until after my trip to Europe had ended. But having experienced an epiphany of sorts in Berlin—namely the desire to move there—I suddenly became much more interested in checking out what the dating scene had to offer.

And there, on one of the first days I was browsing the website with these newfound intentions, was where I encountered Oliver's profile. Naturally, he was beyond my preferred age range, but he was one of the only individuals whose profile seemed *real*. He wrote with a unique voice, and, unlike most of the 20-something men, he didn't attempt to paint himself as more accomplished or put-together than he really was. Plus, he mentioned being green-eyed and left-handed.

Figuring I had nothing to lose, I sent him a message:

Jul 18 – 11:14pm
"I'm also green-eyed and left-handed and think it's amazing, although the only other people who also think that's amazing are people who are green-eyed and left-handed...funny how that works out."

In exactly an hour-and-a-half, he replied. And over the course of the next day, our communication exceeded the mark of 5,000 words shared between us.

Within a matter of weeks, as our communication continued, I began viewing Oliver as a confidant. Furthermore, there was reciprocation in his writing that hinted at intimacy, the kind that I had been missing in my life for a long time. Never at any point did I find myself holding back, and the space at the end of the day where I would write him was my way of de-stressing and getting out all the frustrations, anxieties, excitements, and disappointments.

Our pen-pal-esque relationship continued to evolve over the following months, and we left out no detail in our messages to one another. I knew about the women he occasionally brought home with him after a night out at a bar or club. He filled me in on the affair he was having with a woman only known as M., who invited him over to her flat once a week as part of their friends-with-benefits arrangement. I was privy to the history of his broken family, to the mistakes of his childhood that carried into the present, rendering him incapable of loving someone without subconsciously destroying it. In this way, we were similar. We both wanted love, but neither of us wanted it enough to face our demons, so we settled for mediocre fill-ins.

But unlike past correspondences, I felt like Oliver was filling a void in my emotional life. Our sharing brought us closer, and although there was no physicality involved, at times I felt like he was the other half of an open relationship: Although I dated other men, fucked other men, he was the one I went home to. He was the sole recipient of my real line of thinking. I could be contradictory, I could be confusing, I could be culpable, I could be any number of things, but what it came down to is that he got me.

I like to think that I got him too. In the fall, I sent him a package, complete with a mix CD. Rather than opting for the route of capturing feelings, moods and emotions, I wanted him to receive something that he would thoroughly enjoy.

WE KNOW WHERE WE'RE GOING

Road to Nowhere – **The Talking Heads**
Panic – **The Smiths**
Search and Destroy – **Iggy And The Stooges**
Jeepster – **T. Rex**
Show of Strength – **Echo And The Bunnymen**
Disorder – **Joy Division**
Personality Crisis – **New York Dolls**
The Way We Get By – **Spoon**
After Hours – **The Velvet Underground**
More Than This – **Roxy Music**
Incinerate – **Sonic Youth**
Range Life – **Pavement**
You Really Got Me – **The Kinks**
Freak Scene – **Dinosaur Jr.**
Kiss Off – **Violent Femmes**
Sometimes – **My Bloody Valentine**

And I nailed it. I knew I had succeeded when he sent me an email after receiving the package saying that upon first listen, he knew off the top of his head what every song was, with the exception of one. He also shared his relief that I hadn't included any Bowie, otherwise that would have been the surefire sign that I was inside his head.

In return, Oliver made me a mix of my own. However, he wasn't quite as computer savvy as I was, so in lieu of burning and mailing a CD, he opted to send me a sequence of links to YouTube videos.

LOST IN MUSIC

Love is Strong – **The Rolling Stones**
Strutter – **Kiss**
Seconds – **The Human League**
Almost – **O.M.D.**
Dead Sound – **The Raveonettes**
I Can Hear Music – **The Ronettes**
We're Lost in Music – **Sister Sledge**
Demon Lover – **Shocking Blue**
Kerosene – **Big Black**
Passion (12-inch remix) – **The Flirts**
Falling and Laughing – **Orange Juice**
Ride a White Horse – **Goldfrapp**
Isobel Goudie – **Alex Harvey Band**
Lost in Music – **The Fall**
Fade Into You – **Mazzy Star**
Big City (Everybody I Know Can Be Found Here) –
Spacemen 3
Paris 1919 – **John Cale**

All this talking eventually brought up my planned trip to Germany over the holiday break. Feeling that I'd built up a solid rapport with Oliver, I asked him if I might be able to stay with him for a couple nights while in Berlin for Silvester, or New Year's Eve. He agreed—although, he pointed out, we'd have to share a bed. The notion made me smile more than I thought it would, or should. Especially when he ended his mails with lines like, "let's see if we are compatible—I think so but we only can be sure after meeting eye to eye. But I am optimistic ;-)."

In the days leading up to my visit, Oliver sent me sporadic messages asking about my dietary habits, informing me he'd stocked up on red wine, coffee, and soy milk. Although the content of these paragraph-long logistical emails was strictly business, the quotidian nature of them made me feel strangely closer to him. In some sense, these conversations about daily necessities and routines were just as intimate as the explicit over-sharing of our own lives that had gone on in the months prior. And each time I read one of these emails, my anticipation would grow, because instead of existing as thoughts without a voice, Oliver was about to become a reality. And the burden of that reality was exhilarating.

Yet it wasn't until the morning of the 31st, sitting on the train a few hours outside of Berlin, that my excitement began to manifest itself as nervous unrest. I could feel myself nearly shaking, and my body was overcome with a cold, restless anxiety that wasn't the slightest bit weather-induced. That the train was an hour late didn't assist in curbing the sick feeling in my stomach either.

The feeling expanded as Berlin grew nearer. We were only at the Berlin-Spandau station, still a stop away from the main station, but already I gathered my belongings together and made my way to the exit of the train car, checking myself in the window reflection to make certain I appeared acceptable.

As the train pulled into the Berlin Hauptbahnhof, I began to shake. Looking out the window, I saw the signs for Gleis 11, section D, E, F; these were the platforms where I told Oliver I'd be waiting. In true Deutsche Bahn fashion, the train continued on past where it was supposed to be, finally resting at sections A, B, C. As it slowly pulled in, I saw Oliver, all 6 feet and 3 inches of him, standing exactly where I said I would be. I felt somewhat relieved, for he appeared as nervous as I felt, and just that thought alone set me at ease.

The train came to a stop and the doors opened, and I stepped out more assuredly. Circumventing the crowds of people congregating near the train, I walked to the other side of the platform and made my way toward the back of the train, to where I'd seen Oliver standing.

And in a moment, which felt simultaneously sped up and slowed down, I noticed him not only standing there, but also searching for me. The look on his face communicated worry that perhaps I had stood him up. But then he looked and saw me, a mere couple of meters away, and in the same instant that his eyes demonstrated a hesitative, questioning recognition, I raised my right hand slowly, and signaled to him with a half wave. He nodded his head toward me and I did all I could to keep from beaming with enthusiasm when we began walking to one another.

The welter of emotions taking over blurred my mind, and I still can't remember if I hugged him or just awkwardly said hello. Maybe both.

We began exchanging pleasantries, but the whole time my eyes were fixated on my toes. I was too afraid to meet his eyes— which I could feel were curiously surveying me and sizing me up—for I thought they might reveal all the things that even I didn't know at the time.

Later he would ask me if he looked like I had expected him to, and I had to admit that he perfectly matched up with his photo, nearly to a T. Even taking into consideration how people carry themselves in a way that a photo fails to communicate, he was still just the way I'd had him pegged. And even though I didn't consciously expect him to saunter with a swagger like Keith Richards, moving his hands about as he walked, as I watched him navigate the train station, his way of moving only seemed completely normal, a natural extension of who he was.

After taking a train a few stops away, we transferred to another, eventually ending up at Nordbahnhof, a station a short walk away from his flat. It was only at this point, walking through the halls of the quiet train station that a thought occurred to Oliver.

"Should I carry some of your luggage?"

I smiled and shrugged, handing over my backpack, and he quickly put it over his shoulders and led the way upstairs.

We stepped out into the late-December streets of Berlin, and although my load was considerably lighter and Oliver assured me that the walk was a short one, I took careful steps to avoid the collectives of melting ice on the sidewalks. I'd slipped and fallen a few days earlier while in Cologne, and I remembered the cold, stinging feeling on my upper thigh that persisted for hours after colliding with the hard, wet surface.

Breaking my concentration, Oliver's voice asked me if I recognized where I was. We were in Mitte, I knew that much, but it wasn't a street I ever remembered having walked down on my first visit to Berlin. Looking to my left and then to my right, it occurred to me that there were an unusual amount of tourists grouped alongside the right side of the street. But why? Suddenly it dawned on me that, running alongside the road, there were remnants of the Berlin Wall itself.

"You didn't tell me you live this close to the Mauer," I remarked, as Oliver began to tell me the turn of events that brought him to this apartment a year earlier. Prior to moving to his current location, he'd spent his first 16 years in Berlin in one place.

We turned left down a side street and walked past a few buildings, finally making our way up to the one he lived in. He unlocked it and flipped on the light switch, then started up the steps, stopping at the third floor landing to open the first door to the right.

"Take off your shoes," he sang out as he pulled the keys out of the door and moved inside.

I followed him and stepped out of my snow boots. He took them from me, walking into the bathroom and placing them in the bathtub alongside his own shoes, which were more combat boots than anything else. Then I walked into the room that made up the living area of his flat. Setting my bags down on the closest chair, I glanced outside the windows in front of me. It was just before 4 p.m. and I could see the sun beginning to fall down across the sky.

"Do you want some coffee?"

I glanced to my right; Oliver was standing in the kitchen looking at me inquisitively.

I shrugged my shoulders.

"Why not?"

As he set to work grinding the beans with his grandmother's antique coffee grinder, I took the opportunity to organize my belongings and look around the room. His bed was situated in one corner with a nightstand next to it. Along the wall was a long row of shelves that nearly reached to the ceiling, with thousands of records gracing them. On the floor in front of the shelves were more records. Later I'd ask Oliver what criteria he used to determine which records went on the floor, to which he'd answer that the display consisted of a mix of his most recently purchased albums, rare finds that he would later sell on eBay, and records that he particularly loved at that moment in time.

In the corner facing the window was a simple desk with a computer, sporting a brand new monitor he'd told me about. Next to it, there was a door that led onto the balcony. There were the chairs I'd left my bags on, and then a doorway that opened into the narrow kitchen. As I stepped from the carpet onto the cool linoleum, Oliver looked up and smiled. Standing in the small space was awkward, so at his insistence, I sat at one of the two chairs pushed into the corner table.

Oliver grabbed the French press and pulled out the second chair, ceremoniously sitting down and crossing his right leg across the left. He'd already placed sugar on the table, and looking at it, paused.

"You will want some soy milk," he said, half-question, half-statement.

"Yes, please."

He stood up and opened the refrigerator door, retrieving the milk and placing it next to my mug. It was pale yellow, wide, and shallow, with a smiley face drawn on the side next to some words in German. His own mug was light blue with Tweedy Bird on it, something he told me his younger sister had given him years earlier, when the Berlin Looney Toons store had a going-out-of-business sale.

His attention turned to the press, and after he deemed it sufficiently brewed, Oliver gently pushed down on the plunger, before pouring the coffee into my cup, then his.

We drank our coffee slowly and deliberately, and as I reached the bottom, he refilled it. All the while, we talked, about anything and everything. The purpose of conversation was two-fold. We talked because we were interested in hearing about one another. And we talked because it felt good to do so, after six months of exchanging words on computer screens.

Oliver nonchalantly reached for a nearby tea tin, where he kept his stash of loose-leaf tobacco, and began rolling a cigarette. He kept talking, but I paid more attention to what his hands were doing: the way he pinched the loose leaves between his fingertips, gingerly rolling the paper and licking it to seal the tiny cylinder.

"Time to smoke," he said. "Do you want to come with me or stay in here?"

I stood up wordlessly, following him to the entrance of his flat, where he put on boots and gave me a pair of women's platform sandals to wear. I put on my jacket as he then strode across the room, opening the door to the balcony and holding it open for me.   "Watch your step," he said, and I looked down to avoid tripping on the raised inset of the door. Stepping over it, my feet landed on green Astroturf covering the balcony. Oliver closed the door and stood next to me. He lit his cigarette, and as he took a drag, he pointed out across the landscape toward a building half a block away.

"That's a Catholic Hospital. Sometimes I see nuns walking back and forth," he said, moving his hand in a sideways motion. "It's fucking weird," he added, shaking his head as though in disbelief.

I leaned on the green bar running the length of the balcony, my forearms resting on the cold metal, my hands hanging over below. This would become our routine for the next two days: coffee, conversation, cigarettes, repeat.

Back inside, we took our shoes off, reconvening in the kitchen. We drank more coffee. Outside, people in the streets began setting off fireworks at regular intervals, the trail of their lights illuminating the overcast sky. Initially, every time one went off, I'd sit up with a start, although it was only a matter of time before the sound of them erupting faded from the foreground of my consciousness.

We talked for hours, about everything we'd talked about before. It was exactly the same, except that instead of being separated by 5,000 miles, we were directly across the table from one another. And now I had a voice to fit with the words I'd become so accustomed to. I watched as he laughed and his eyes lit up, the skin around the edges crinkling up as he smiled. I noted that as he talked, his hands seemed to be telling a story all their own, moving to and fro, acting out where words failed.

I made fun of his English, which was nearly immaculate in spite of his thick, German accent. He defended himself, telling me: "My English is a mixtape, you know," explaining that it was a mixture of British and American words with a German accent.

The most noticeable discrepancy in his speaking was his pronunciation of certain sounds. Every time he used a word that began with a "w" he pronounced it as a "v," at which point I would always laugh and then correct him.

"Wir können auf Deutsch sprechen," I said, suggesting we talk in German.

"You sound like a Polish used car salesman when you speak German," was his retort.

Once the coffee was gone, Oliver suggested we have dinner. He turned down my offer to help, so I sat at the table watching him while he prepared the pasta. His kitchen was too small for more than one person to comfortably move around in anyway. As the noodles cooked, he began hand-washing the dishes.

"I only have two bowls," he explained. "We need them to eat."

"You're such a boy," I said in response.

He stopped and looked at me, head cocked sideways, as if to ask what I meant.

"Nevermind," I sighed, smiling at him.

After dinner, we moved out of the kitchen to the room. I sat down on the ground while Oliver lit candles and turned off the lights, eventually taking a place across from me with a carafe of wine and two glasses.

For the next six hours, we sat on the floor, drinking three bottles of wine together, listening to records and sharing parts of ourselves. For all the disclosing we had done over the Internet, I was afraid that things would be strange, that sharing would be difficult. Yet sitting there in that room with him, it dawned on me that our evening together was the most emotionally intimate experience I had had with someone in years. I wasn't afraid of being judged for what I thought or did, and I wanted to connect with him. More than anything, I knew deep down that, in spite of my bad judgment calls in the past, Oliver wasn't someone who would hurt me, intentionally or not.

Suddenly, a barrage of fireworks went off in the distance.

"Happy New Year," we said to one another, staring out the window at the various shows going on all around us.

Oliver stood up and walked over to his records, pulling out Girls' *Album*, which had come out in 2010. The band was from San Francisco, so although I knew them, I was surprised he was so familiar with their music as well.

Next he pulled out an original pressing of Trio's 1981 self-titled album.

"Look at the back," he said as he placed the record on the turntable. "They put their phone number on the cover."

We drank our way through that album until it ended, when we decided it was time to go to bed.

After brushing my teeth and changing into my pajamas, I walked out in the room and got into bed. Already under the covers, Oliver began laughing.

"This is the most clothed a girl in my bed has ever been," he exclaimed.

"I get cold at night," I shot back, but proceeded to take off my sweatshirt.

Lying down on my side facing him, Oliver pulled the blanket around us and nestled up closely to me, the warmth of his nearly naked body arousing me. He was wearing only underwear, and although I was undeniably attracted to him, the thought of something happening between the two of us had never occurred to me during our time together until that moment.

We put our arms around one another, and as we drew closer, I smiled in the darkness. Closing my eyes, I could hear the 2 a.m. fireworks still going off, but now, they sounded like peaceful murmurs.

I woke up the following morning to the sun. Gently, Oliver rolled onto his side, placing his arm around me once again. I backed myself up closer to his bent frame, folding my body into his, and as his hand touched mine, I opened my fingers so that ours would interlace. Then I fell back into a light sleep, dozing on and off for the next couple hours.

When I finally woke up, I rolled onto my stomach, and seeing that Oliver was awake, I spoke.

"I'm sorry for stealing your pillow all night."

"I don't need a pillow. But you did steal the blanket."

"I didn't mean to! You should have stolen it back!"

"I should probably just get another blanket."

"So buy another one."

"That's something my mother should do, not me."

Our banter went back and forth, until Oliver eventually gave up.

He got out of bed and headed for the bathroom, returning with the bathrobe I'd seen hanging on the back of the door earlier. It was a terry-cloth material, with red, blue, yellow, and green vertical stripes, something his father had given him. Putting it on, he walked into the kitchen to make some coffee. Moments later, I joined him. Sitting at the table, cross-legged and messy-haired, I rubbed the sleep out of my eyes while he talked.

That was the thing about Oliver. He talked. A lot. I never got the suspicion that he talked simply because he loved to hear himself. Instead, he talked because he was curious and full of wonder. And in some sense, I got the feeling that he was lonely. It wasn't that he was dissatisfied, but he wanted to connect with other people on a deeper level, and our time together afforded him that.

"*Klingelinggggg!*"

The harsh sound of his phone interrupted my thoughts. Oliver strode across the room to answer the phone, which was placed upon the top of a bookshelf. In a moment, I was overwhelmed with a rush of German words, and as I listened to him talk, I was again overcome with a sense of excitement from the most unlikely of places. Of all things, listening to him speak in German turned me on. I couldn't explain it, but I didn't mind it either.

New Year's Day passed by in a blur. We spent the day doing insignificant things, albeit things that only served to deepen the nature of our relationship. Mostly, we talked. And it was there, in the mundane, that we found an appreciation for one another. He was impressed by my knowledge of music; in his experience, girls knew nothing about or how to appreciate records or music in general. As for me, someone who values communication above all else in a relationship, I was fascinated by how much he disclosed about himself. There was no topic too secret or sacred.

"You know when you said I look my age yesterday?" Oliver asked suddenly as he was getting dressed.

"Yes… "

"I have something to confess."

I raised my eyebrow a bit and gave him a questioning look.

"What exactly do you mean?"

"I'm not really 36."

"No?! So, you're…?" I let my silence hang like a question mark.

He finished buttoning his jeans, then grabbed his wallet, pulled out his ID card, and triumphantly handed it to me. Finding the birthdate, I saw he was born in 1970.

"So that means..." I began, silently doing the math. "You're 40!"

"Yes!"

"So why lie? Forty isn't bad."

"But it is!" he exclaimed. "No one is interested in you if you're 40. But drop your age a couple years and things change."

"So what do you do if you meet a woman, but she thinks you're 36. Do you eventually tell her? After how long? And how does she feel about you lying?"

Oliver simply shrugged.

As for me, I wasn't shocked so much as amused, and made certain to bring up the minor untruth throughout the remainder of the day.

As dusk set in upon us again, Oliver suggested we go get some food and drinks for the evening.

"I want pizza," he said. "Pizza and beer. Does that sound good?"

"Of course."

We bundled up and headed outside. The temperature was warmer than the day before, inching slightly above 0 degrees Celsius. The snow had begun melting and was a mixture of ice and slush. We walked carefully to the Nordbahnhof train station down the street, getting off a few stops later at Friedrichstraße, one of the larger train stations, containing a grocery store in its underground shelter. We walked in and I followed him through the narrow rows, down to the beer aisle, where he picked out six large bottles of Pilsner. Then we stopped by the frozen foods, picking out a cheese pizza for me and a tuna fish one for himself.

"Tuna fish?" I asked incredulously. "That's gross."

"What? Tuna fish pizza is the best."

I shook my head, grinning.

"You Germans and your tuna fish in everything," I said. "That's just wrong."

Our new purchases in hand, we made our way out of the store.

"Want to walk back?" Oliver asked. "It's only a few stops."

"Sure," I replied.

We set out down the road. Oliver commented on how surprised he was to see so many people out on New Year's Day, but I wasn't listening so much as I was taking in everything surrounding me. Although I knew we were in Germany, it was easy to forget that back at Oliver's flat. In fact, spending time with him made it easy for me to forget most things. With him, I was truly living in the moment.

Oliver's complaints about the slushy ice broke my thoughts.

"Let's take the train after all," he said, crossing the road toward the Oranienburger Straße station.

A stop, and a short walk later, we were back in Oliver's kitchen, waiting for our food to cook. His oven was only large enough to cook one pizza at a time, and mine was first. When it was warmed, he put it on a plate and set it in front of me, then turned to put his pizza in the oven.

"What are you waiting for?" he asked, looking at my untouched food.

"I'm waiting for your food to be ready too," I replied.

As we waited, I noticed he had set out two knives by his plate, same as the evening before.

"Why do you have two knives out?" I questioned.

"I need them with every meal, for a balance of power."

A few minutes later, he took his pizza out of the oven.

"Guten Appetit!" we said to one another.

We spoke about our plans for the following day, a Sunday. In the afternoon, I was planning on heading to Steglitz, to meet up with Matthias, a couch-surfer whose place I was staying at. Meanwhile, Oliver wanted to partake of his weekly ritual of buying records on Sunday.

"I'm going to the flea market where I'll allow myself to buy one record only," he said methodically. "And next week I won't allow myself to go, because it is my birthday and I'm hoping my friends will buy me records instead."

"Do you think they will?" I asked.

"Probably not. I wish they would. Tobi knows what to get me, but he's in Austria. And John will likely get me some hipster record. He's 25 you know, so he's always listening to whatever is cool. He's really big on what I like to call 'McCartney Melodies.'" Oliver laughed. "The rest of my friends will probably buy me boring things, like pots and pans. Puh."

Our conversation launched into a discussion of record criteria, which led to us moving into his room and reconvening our positions from the night before. I sat cross-legged against a chair and he put some pillows on the floor, resting his arms on them and extending his legs out. We drank the bottles of Pilsner, extending a Prost to one another with each new bottle. Our soundtrack this evening included the new Crystal Castles album, which then launched into what Oliver described as "jangle-pop"—New Zealand-based bands like the Clean and the Chills. When he played "Pink Frost" by the Chills, I could actually feel myself getting the chills, overcome with the haunting sounds and beautiful melody.

Other things he introduced me to: the Undertones' "Teenage Kicks," the Television Personalities, and another German band: the 39 Clocks. When he got to Led Zeppelin, though, I began to object.

"I can't ever get into them. Not because I don't like them, but they have so much music. I don't know where to begin."

"Begin at the beginning," he said.

We went to bed earlier that night than the one before. The next morning, I slept in, waking up to the sound of Oliver at his computer, clicking with his mouse and drinking coffee. He must have heard me stir, because he turned around and, seeing I was awake, began talking to me. I stayed in bed, not moving, and he kept talking, launching into a diatribe about the most recent email he'd received.

"You shouldn't have woken up. Now I won't stop talking," he said.

I smiled through sleepy eyes but said nothing.

"So when do you need to leave?" he asked.

"I have to be at Matthias' place around 3," I responded. "Help me figure out how to get there?"

I read the address to him as he typed it into his browser. After a few minutes of clicking, he scribbled down directions in my notebook, and subsequently dictated them to me verbally.

"What are you doing after you get there?" he asked.

"He's going to let me in, then go play Snooker. I am meeting up with him and his friends tonight to play pool."

"Want to come back then, and hang out?"

"Sure! That would be nice."

So it was decided. And once I was dressed and packed, we set out for the Nordbahnhof train station, with Oliver repeating the directions he'd written down, instructing me once again how to get there.

"Get on the S1 and take it maybe 10 stops. Get off at Feuerbachstraße. Then it's a five-minute walk from there."

I nodded and got onto my train.

The directions were exactly right, and I found Matthias' place in no time. He let me in, gave me a quick tour, handed me a house key and pointed to a post-it note where he'd drawn a map of where to meet him later and how to get there.

"But don't come until after 8 p.m.," he said, noting that his Snooker game—about which he was particularly serious—could not be interrupted.

I said goodbye. As the door closed, I surveyed my surroundings. To the left was the doorway of the room I was staying in. It was stocked with books and travel guides, dictionaries in multiple languages, games, a laptop for guests to use, and a piece of paper with the wireless network and password were written.

I set my belongings down and pulled out my laptop, beginning a new blog entry about my experiences of the past few days. It felt strange for me to be typing on a computer, reading my social media comments from friends, catching up on news from back home. The forty-eight hours with Oliver were like a vacuum of time, where I lost track of everything that existed outside the two of us.

Just then, my phone beeped. Looking down, I saw that Oliver had sent me a text message, to check in, and asking when I'd be back.

"I'm here," I responded. "Maybe an hour, or a little bit longer?"

"OK. I'll take a bath now. Just ring when you arrive."

An hour-and-a-half had passed by the time I made it back to the middle of Berlin, and even though it was dark and cold and I was alone, I walked assuredly from the station to Oliver's flat, a path that already felt like second nature to me.

I rang his bell and he let me in, and as I began up the flight of stairs, the hall light switched on and I rounded the steps to see Oliver standing in the doorway, looking at me keenly.

I entered his place just as I had two days before, but now I felt certain, sure of myself.

"What do we want to drink?" he said, half-asking me, half-talking to himself. "I don't have any more alcohol since we drank it all..."

His voice trailed off as he hunched over, searching through the cabinet under his countertops.

"Aha! I found something!"

He pulled out a bottle of white Swedish glögg and held it up triumphantly.

"Let's try this, shall we?"

He set out two mugs and began to heat the clear liquid in a pot.

As we waited for it to be ready, we talked about the two hours we'd been apart, both of us agreeing that it was a strange feeling to be functioning in the world without the other there. However, while for him it made him turn his attention outward to how he could make his everyday interactions feel more intense like ours, I turned inward, desperately speculating about what it meant about him, about us, about me.

Those last two hours together flew by too quickly, and before long we were once again at Nordbahnhof, for the final time. The plan was for him to accompany me two stops. He would get off and have his weekly ritual of a drink or two to bid farewell to the weekend. Meanwhile, I'd stay on and make my way back to the south of the city to meet up with Matthias.

As the S-Bahn pulled into our second stop, Oliver rose to leave. I stood up to hug him, feeling more than a tinge of sadness.

"It's not goodbye," he said to me, maintaining a hopeful sense. "I will see you when you move here soon."

I sat back down and he stepped off. As the train pulled away, I looked out the window to see him glance over his shoulder. My feet were resting on the seat across from me. His eyes looked at them and he shook his head, reprimanding me. I laughed and moved them down quickly. He smiled once again and then looked away. That was the last I saw of him.

Our correspondence continued after I left and flew to Sweden, still on vacation but removed from Germany, and from Oliver, and not yet back in normal life, so I could finally process it. In the following week, we resumed our exchange of emails, including the one in which he asked if I was in love with him. And while he understood what I was saying and acknowledged that something intense had transpired between us, it seemed to me that things would remain at that level, where I was the girl who he could talk to more freely than with any other girl, but who he would never—could never—be with. It was, he acknowledged, as if he could only be with women who didn't intellectually stimulate or challenge him. And in reverse, the women who made the synapses in his brain fire with stimulation—the women like me—could only exist in that other kind of space. There was no room for crossover.

This principle was solidified sometime in February.

It was a Wednesday evening, and he had gone on a date with an opera singer from New York who not only had written him through the dating website, but was living a few miles away from him in Berlin. She initiated contact and the two met up in a bar. In the week prior to their getting together, Oliver excitedly wrote me, saying how he was hopeful and curious about this new prospect. And I was genuinely thrilled for him, wishing that it would go well.

So naturally, I was surprised to receive another email from Oliver when he should have been on the date, telling me that he ended it early to go home and listen to the new Twin Shadow record. Which was only typical of him.

But it was the final line of the email that affected me.

"In the end I struggled to find things to say," he said of the date. "Which is something I never experienced with you."

Upon reading those words, my heart stopped.

I realized then my role in his life. It wasn't a romantic, life-changing love. But I was one of those people who would always be there, who would connect with him on the level that others didn't, or couldn't. And as much as I was attracted to him, as many reasons as there were to pursue him, and as well as a romantic relationship might have turned out, that's not what our relationship would be. It just wasn't in the cards for us.

SMITH

"I don't want to be married anymore. Not to you, not to anyone."

With those words, Smith took out his carabiner, removed the car key and the apartment key from the rest, and handed them over. As a final gesture, he took off his wedding ring and dropped it into my hand. Then he walked away, silently.

It was June 3. We had been married for 885 days and just like that, it was coming to an end. Of course, it wasn't really just like that, because it had been building up from the beginning, intensified over the final few months. Like many things that fall apart, there were indicators leading up to the dissolution of our marriage long before the breaking point arrived.

The truth is, I married someone I loved, but love is not enough to make a relationship work. In our case, something fundamental was broken from the start, and it was trust.

Smith had been cheating on me since the beginning, and I knew it. The early revelations were explained away as girls he was dating before we met but never officially broke it off with. Later in the relationship, as the wedding came closer, he explained them away as emotional connections, but never something physical. On and on went the list of excuses, and more and more I lied to myself that it didn't matter, that he was marrying me after all.

For some reason, these indiscretions never threatened me, perhaps because I knew about them. But it was the lie that I could not corner him in that scared me the most. For a few weeks prior, he acted sketchy and shifty, and when I confronted him directly, asking him "Did you fuck her?" he was defiant rather than in denial.

"That's none of your business," he had replied. It was a response that, although it confirmed my worst fear, was still lacking in substantial evidence required to move forward.

The day he left me was the day I finally had the proof. My raging jealousy, unstable emotions, and unfounded suspicious could no longer be brushed aside as signs pointing to my insecurity, for I had the phone bills documenting late-night texting, the e-mails professing her love for him, the corroborating admissions from family members and friends that they hadn't been with him when he claimed they had.

And so I told him that I knew, and while I chose to stay and fight for our relationship, it was a no-brainer for him: flight. After all, if he truly didn't want to be married as he claimed, this revelation gave him the out that he so desperately wanted.

After he left, I called my parents, and through choked-up words, told them what happened. They insisted I shouldn't be alone and made the 30-minute drive from their home in Santa Rosa to mine in Petaluma, bringing me back home with them.

Later that night, friends came over with beer and chocolate, offering their condolences and confusion. But the confusion wasn't regarding us breaking up so much as how it happened.

"I always thought you would be the one to leave him," said one friend.

And it could have been foreshadowing, because although he instigated our end, I was the one left to deal with cleaning up the mess left in its place.

The first thing I did was pack up all the love notes and letters, the lunch bag post-its and refrigerator reminders, the ticket stubs and postcards, and put them in a box. At first, it was a simple task, because I kept them in obvious places, like my wallet or sock drawer. But as time went on, they slowly revealed themselves to me in the unassuming locations. One was at the bottom of my purse, another under the bed, a folded-up piece of paper in the pocket of a sweatshirt. And I tortured myself, reading those notes one by one as I came across them, their very existence belying my reality.

To that box of words I added photo booth strips, the ones of us kissing that we took every year at the fair. The half-eaten containers of orange Tic Tacs, his favorite candy, went in there too. And while I couldn't listen to music in the weeks that followed, I still took the CDs that reminded me of him—albums by the Black Heart Procession and the Velvet Teen—as well as mixtapes I'd made him over the years, and added them to the collection, one by one. Eventually, as I began incorporating music back into my life, the songs that once seemed to be the most perfect manifestation of my love for him were rotated out to make way for songs with more fitting themes: of hopelessness, of breakups, of loneliness, of despair. Listening to anything that I remotely associated with him made me sob uncontrollably, regardless of my surroundings. The music had no regard for my feelings and made no distinction between the public and the private spheres. I could be in the grocery store, driving on the freeway, or in a movie theater, and upon hearing a song, the association would made me break down and cry.

All these things existed in the back of my closet, hidden away but still painfully within reach. And I knew they were there, but for the most part, chose to ignore them.

Of course, there were other things too big to place inside of a shoebox, like bottles of Jameson that we used to drink from those first few months together, the grill from the balcony where we had BBQs, my baby blue Brother typewriter which gave birth to all the love notes. These things were relegated to cluttered shelves and corners, and although I saw them regularly, I refused to enjoy them.

I began erasing evidence of our online existence as a couple: photos were taken down from social networking sites; passwords were changed. But as much as I tried, certain things couldn't be avoided. I had forgotten about our movie queue, until I logged in to request a video and saw everything he'd picked, still waiting patiently in line. I would feel OK until an email arrived, reminding him to pay his credit card bill, or a notice that his new phone bill was ready to be viewed. Even though he got stuck with the payments, the phones, the numbers, I still got the emails, arriving in my inbox like a last word.

Others were things I began neglecting. All the plants died because I gave up on watering them. For the most part, the cats didn't suffer. Two of them had loved me the best, and another one could go either way, so they didn't notice that Smith was gone. Or if they did, it didn't affect their routine. Only one, the young black cat, seemed to be searching for him constantly. While it didn't manifest itself in any sort of detrimental way, I would later realize that subconsciously I had neglected that cat, denied him affection, pushed him away and at times despised him, because he was so clearly aware of the lack that I desperately wanted to conceal, and reminded me of it regularly.

There were places I associated with him that I no longer wanted to visit, or even see. Never again would I eat at an A&W, because it was where we went for root beer floats during those hot summers spent in Sacramento. Never again would I stay at a bed and breakfast, because it was where we went on romantic getaways. Never again would I eat at Hallie's Diner, or Mr. Mom's Café, because these were our regular breakfast spots, and I was all too certain he was still eating at them, taking my replacement there. Instead, I was forced to find new places to visit, to eat, to see shows, to stay. And anyplace would suffice—anyplace that didn't remind me of him.

Of course, the slightly more intangible things were there too, which were the hardest to ignore, for they uncontrollably reappeared in my mind at inopportune times. I changed the sheets the day after he left, because I foolishly thought it would eliminate the scent of him. Where I once slept cuddled up and close to him, I began to hate the thought of sleeping next to someone. Instead I relished the queen-size bed to myself. But where I had reclaimed the bedroom for myself again, I nearly forgot about the smell of cigarette that lingered always on his clothes, his fingers, and his lips. And sitting at the bar or walking downtown, the smell would drift across my path, reminding me of what it was like to be next to him.

In spite of all I did to push Smith out of my mind, there were other things I did—some consciously, some not—that prevented me from forgetting him completely. It didn't help that I still wore my rings for months afterward. Removing them made me feel naked, so I kept them on, and even though I had moved them to different, less significant fingers, they still served as a reminder of a life with him. I didn't cut off contact with him either, and the text messages we shared—whether he was fighting with me over who got what or telling me in a moment of weakness that he still loved me—reinforced the illusion that somehow things were "OK," that we were just on some kind of break, that the actuality of my situation was temporary. And for months after, I still lived in the apartment we shared, only realizing a little too late that the bad energy was stifling me, because every corner of that flat was somewhere we had cooked or cleaned, talked or watched TV, fought or fucked.

Eventually, with time, these things began to fade. The memories became duller, less meaningful, until the objects and places and sensations that once defined my life were replaced and made obsolete and forgotten.

The most challenging thing was to let go of the music. The rest I was able to either immediately hide away in boxes, or slowly reinvent through experience, allowing new memories to write over the old, to erase any previous emotional attachment. But the music was special—it always had been for me—exactly because it said everything I couldn't say on my own, and I couldn't help but be reminded of that. He'd taken away so much of what I once thought was mine, and I refused to let it control my life. I decided to reclaim it through a mix.

I've made hundreds of mixes in my life. Their lengths, musical styles, and lyrical themes were all different. Suffice to say, plenty of them were for crushes and lovers, but all of them were strangely lacking in real intention. I attribute this to perspective. These were collections of songs that I compiled to create and convey an overall sentiment. I spent hours carefully crafting each mix, but they all ultimately served as vague testaments to feelings that weren't fully flushed out, or sincere.

Suddenly, when I was forced to make a mixtape from the standpoint of a love I'd had to let go of, I realized the power of a mix. The one in which I felt real love, where every single word of every single song was specifically chosen to encapsulate my feelings, paradoxically came into being on the outskirts of love. And I finally began to comprehend that it is precisely when someone is no longer in love, not merging with another— when someone is standing in the blank space that makes up the aftermath of forever—that they feel the most intense love. So instead, where Smith traded one warm body for another, I traded my love for one, final mixtape.

I LOVE YOU MORE THAN YOU KNOW (AND THAT WON'T MAKE THINGS RIGHT)

Woke Up New – **The Mountain Goats**
The Ghost of What Should Have Been – **Owen**
Heart Without a Home – **The Black Heart Procession**
The End – **Track Star**
Falling Out of Love at This Volume – **Bright Eyes**
Hold Me Close – **Lucero**
International You Day – **Tony Sly**
Fast Asleep In Her Arms – **The New Trust**
Maybe You're Gone – **Sondre Lerche**
Ferocious Love – **Aloha**
The Ice Is Getting Thinner – **Death Cab For Cutie**
The Golden Band – **American Analog Set**
October Leaves – **The Good Life**

ACKNOWLEDGEMENTS

Writing a book has long been a dream of mine, and now that it's finally a reality, I want to express my gratitude to everyone who has contributed both to the journey and the end result.

In particular, I want to thank my parents, for instilling and nurturing a love of the written word in me from a very young age, and for raising me to believe in my own abilities.

Thank you to my editors, who, in their various capacities, helped refine and polish this book into something better than I could have created on my own.

I am particularly indebted to Noelle Oxenhandler, who both challenged my writing and inspired its growth, and whose poignant insight shaped the overall storyline significantly.

To all the people at Microcosm, including Lauren Hage, Meggyn Pomerleau, Tim Wheeler, Nathan Thomas, Erik Spellmeyer, and Jeff Hayes, thank you for your editing, designing, promoting, selling, and shipping, among the other countless behind-the-scenes work you do.

Big ups go out to Avi Ehrlich for being reachable at all hours of the night and dispensing seasoned and invaluable advice.

I also want to send out love to Christine Davids, Molly Mande, Emily Hostutler, Erica Tom, and Anne Convery for always being available to talk out my process, test drive my writing, or get a post-seminar beer.

I am grateful to Elia Leigh Inglis (LP) for many things, but mostly for helping me realize how lucky I am to be able to fall in love more than once.

To Joe Biel, thank you for your encouragement, support, and transparency. More importantly, I am beholden to you for seeing my vision, believing in it, and ultimately, taking a risk on me.

Finally, all my love to M., my real-life happy ending. Thank you for loving me endlessly, respecting my personhood, and always making me laugh. You are the end that justifies my means.